BARRON'S BOOK NOTES

KURT VONNEGUT'S

Slaughterhouse-Five

BARRON'S BOOK NOTES

KURT VONNEGUT'S

Slaughterhouse-Five

BY

William Bly
Assistant Professor of Drama
New York University

SERIES COORDINATOR
Murray Bromberg
Principal, Wang High School of Queens
Holliswood, New York

Past President
High School Principals Association of New York City

BARRON'S EDUCATIONAL SERIES, INC.
Woodbury, New York • London • Toronto • Sydney

ACKNOWLEDGMENTS

Our thanks to Milton Katz and Julius Liebb for their advisory assistance on the *Book Notes* series.

All inquiries should be addressed to:
Barron's Educational Series, Inc.
113 Crossways Park Drive
Woodbury, New York 11797

Library of Congress Catalog Card No. 85-3933

International Standard Book No. 0-7641-9123-3

Library of Congress Cataloging in Publication Data
Bly, William.
　　Kurt Vonnegut's Slaughterhouse five.

　　(Barron's book notes)
　　Bibliography, p. 102
　　Summary: A guide to reading "Slaughterhouse Five" with a critical and appreciative mind encouraging analysis of plot, style, form, and structure. Also includes background on the author's life and times, sample tests, term paper suggestions, and a reading list.
　　1. Vonnegut, Kurt. Slaughterhouse-five. [1. Vonnegut, Kurt. Slaughterhouse-five.　2. American literature— History and criticism]　I. Title.　II. Series.
PS3572.O5S632　1985　　　813'.54　　　85-3933
ISBN 0-7641-9123-3

PRINTED IN THE UNITED STATES OF AMERICA

567　　550　　987654321

CONTENTS

ADVISORY BOARD

HOW TO USE THIS BOOK

You have to know how to approach literature in order to get the most out of it. This *Barron's Book Notes* volume follows a plan based on methods used by some of the best students to read a work of literature.

Begin with the guide's section on the author's life and times. As you read, try to form a clear picture of the author's personality, circumstances, and motives for writing the work. This background usually will make it easier for you to hear the author's tone of voice, and follow where the author is heading.

Then go over the rest of the introductory material—such sections as those on the plot, characters, setting, themes, and style of the work. Underline, or write down in your notebook, particular things to watch for, such as contrasts between characters and repeated literary devices. At this point, you may want to develop a system of symbols to use in marking your text as you read. (Of course, you should only mark up a book you own, not one that belongs to another person or a school.) Perhaps you will want to use a different letter for each character's name, a different number for each major theme of the book, a different color for each important symbol or literary device. Be prepared to mark up the pages of your book as you read. Put your marks in the margins so you can find them again easily.

Now comes the moment you've been waiting for—the time to start reading the work of literature. You may want to put aside your *Barron's Book Notes* volume until you've read the work all the way through. Or you may want to alternate, reading the *Book Notes* analysis of each section as soon as you have finished reading the corresponding part of the original. Before you move on, reread crucial passages you don't fully understand. (Don't take this guide's analysis for granted—make up your own mind as to what the work means.)

Once you've finished the whole work of literature, you may want to review it right away, so you can firm up your ideas about what it means. You may want to leaf through the book concentrating on passages you marked in reference to one character or one theme. This is also a good time to reread the *Book Notes* introductory material, which pulls together insights on specific topics.

When it comes time to prepare for a test or to write a paper, you'll already have formed ideas about the work. You'll be able to go back through it, refreshing your memory as to the author's exact words and perspective, so that you can support your opinions with evidence drawn straight from the work. Patterns will emerge, and ideas will fall into place; your essay question or term paper will almost write itself. Give yourself a dry run with one of the sample tests in the guide. These tests present both multiple-choice and essay questions. An accompanying section gives answers to the multiple-choice questions as well as suggestions for writing the essays. If you have to select a term paper topic, you may choose one from the list of suggestions in this book. This guide also provides you with a reading list, to help you when you start research for a term paper, and a selection of provocative comments by critics, to spark your thinking before you write.

THE AUTHOR AND HIS TIMES

In 1968, the year Kurt Vonnegut, Jr., was writing *Slaughterhouse-Five*, the war in Vietnam was at its height. Each evening it invaded millions of American living rooms on the television news, and what viewers saw of the conflict night after night made them worried and uneasy about what was taking place. Opinion polls showed that most Americans were then in favor of the war, but a wave of antiwar protest had welled up across the country, mainly on college campuses. Peaceful demonstrations gave way to riots as hostility deepened between prowar and antiwar factions.

And there was violence of another kind that year. In the spring, two prominent figures were assassinated: first Dr. Martin Luther King, Jr., the inspirational leader of the civil rights movement, then Senator Robert F. Kennedy, the leading Democratic candidate for president, who was running on an antiwar platform. Americans were shocked by these brutal killings, and they began to share with the war protesters a general mood of anger and frustration.

For Kurt Vonnegut in 1968, the atrocities of the war in Vietnam had a deeper significance. Twenty-three years earlier, he had been a soldier in the last months of World War II. As a prisoner of war, he was in Dresden, Germany, on the night of February 13, 1945, when Allied bombers attacked so fiercely that they created a great fire-storm that incinerated the entire city. Some 135,000 people died in the raid, perhaps twice the number of people killed in Hiroshima when the first atom bomb was dropped there about six months later.

Vonnegut spent that night with other POWs and their guards in an underground shelter. When it was possible to leave the shelter the next afternoon, he saw the aftermath of the fire-storm. The city looked like a desolate moonscape: nothing moved anywhere.

For years Vonnegut wanted to tell the story of his Dresden experience, and in Chapter 1 of *Slaughterhouse-Five* he describes the difficulties he had trying to write about it. By 1968 America's escalation of the war in Vietnam and the growing protest against the war had added to his sense of urgency about completing the book. Vonnegut's other writings show that he identified strongly with the younger generation's antiwar and antiestablishment attitudes. If ever he was going to write his antiwar book, 1968 was surely the time to do it.

Vonnegut's "modern ideas" go all the way back to his childhood in Indianapolis, Indiana, where he was born—appropriately—on Armistice Day, November 11, 1922. His parents came from three generations of prosperous and cultured German-Americans, and they instilled in their youngest child their own values of pacifism and humanistic atheism. From his mother Kurt learned a love of the arts, but he tried to follow his father's advice that science was the career of the future. His older brother was already a successful physicist when Vonnegut went to Cornell in 1940 and majored in biochemistry. But then America entered World War

II, and in 1943 Vonnegut joined the army. After a brief study of engineering at Carnegie Tech, he was sent to Europe. There he served as an infantry scout until he was captured by Germans following the Battle of the Bulge. Vonnegut's experience as a prisoner of war forms the basis of Billy Pilgrim's Dresden story in *Slaughterhouse-Five*.

After the war, Vonnegut married a childhood sweetheart and enrolled in the University of Chicago graduate school to study anthropology. Apparently he still believed he wanted to be a scientist. He wrote a master's thesis on the stories of different peoples of the world, showing that many of these stories were similar in structure even though the people who wrote them couldn't possibly have known anything about each other. The thesis was rejected, and Vonnegut quit school to go to work for General Electric in Schenectady, New York. His job in public relations involved explaining and justifying to the public the work of a large scientific corporation. Much of what Vonnegut considers the hypocrisy involved in presenting a good image (the main function of public relations) appears in *Slaughterhouse-Five* as "official" rationalizations for disasters such as Hiroshima and the firebombing of Dresden.

While he was at General Electric, Vonnegut began writing fiction, and in 1950 he "dropped out" to become a full-time writer. His first novel, *Player Piano* (1952), is a futuristic satire of the dog-eat-dog mentality of the corporate world he had tried to fit into for three years.

Thus began what Vonnegut calls his "scrawny years," when he supported his family (and financed his novel-writing) by selling short stories to popular magazines. He admits that many of these stories—most of them are science fiction—are slick, built around a clever gimmick, yet they always uphold such solid American values as the nuclear family and the good guys winning in the end.

His second novel, *The Sirens of Titan* (1959), is also in the science fiction mold, but it is so farfetched that it is a parody of mainstream science fiction. In it, aliens manipulate all of human history in order to deliver a spare part to one of their stranded astronauts. The home planet of the aliens is Tralfamadore, one of the principal settings in *Slaughterhouse-Five*.

Vonnegut's third novel, *Mother Night* (1961), hasn't a trace of science fiction in it. It's the story of Howard W. Campbell, Jr. (who also turns up in *Slaughterhouse-Five*), a brilliant Nazi propagandist who is actually an American spy. While barely mentioning Dresden, *Mother Night* profiles the "military manner" of thinking that Vonnegut encountered as an American soldier in World War II, and he returns to this subject in Chapter 9 of *Slaughterhouse-Five*.

None of his early novels brought Vonnegut much attention or helped much to support his family. By now he had moved his family to Cape Cod, where he supplemented his income from writing by selling cars and doing odd jobs. In 1957 his sister Alice died of cancer at the age of forty, just two days after her husband was killed in a train wreck. (The two catastrophes coming so close together perhaps inspired Vonnegut, in *Slaughterhouse-Five*, to have the death of Billy Pilgrim's wife occur while he is in the hospital recovering from the plane crash.) The Vonneguts adopted three of Alice's children, adding them to their own family of three children. The increased financial strain, coupled with the lack of recognition as a writer, must have been enormously discouraging.

The next two novels began to change all that. *Cat's Cradle* (1963), a grim fantasy about the end of the world, and *God Bless You, Mr. Rosewater* (1965), in which the *Slaughterhouse* characters Eliot Rosewater and Kilgore Trout first appear, at least earned some attention from a handful of critics. And enough of Vonnegut's fellow writers now admired him that he was invited to lecture at the famous Writers Workshop at the University of Iowa. Finally, he won a Guggenheim fellowship, and it enabled him to revisit Dresden in 1967—a trip he describes in the first and last chapters of *Slaughterhouse-Five*. He finished the book the following year, and it was published early in 1969.

Before *Slaughterhouse-Five*, Vonnegut's books had been popular mainly on college campuses and among the liberal communities of New York and San Francisco. This allowed most "experts" on American fiction to dismiss him as a "cult" author. But the appearance of *Slaughterhouse-Five* set off a frenzy of critical appraisal that treated Vonnegut as a serious writer for the first time. Long articles appeared in major magazines and newspapers across the country. Book clubs scrambled to get their hands on the novel. Hollywood optioned the film rights. Vonnegut's five earlier novels were reissued, and critics began to chart the development of his artistic vision through his works.

Not all the appraisal was positive. One reviewer dismissed Vonnegut's writing as "a series of narcissistic giggles," while others deplored his pacifism as being adolescent or downright un-American.

But the majority of critical opinion was favorable, and it remains so today. Many critics claim that Vonnegut's most lasting contribution to American fiction is his innovative style, the "telegraphic-schizophrenic manner" of storytelling he developed for *Slaughterhouse-Five*. Others believe he is more important as a satirist of American life, and they rank him with Sinclair Lewis and Mark Twain. For these reasons, Vonnegut is generally regarded as among the most influential (and popular) American novelists to emerge in the 1960s and 1970s.

THE NOVEL

The Plot

Billy Pilgrim, like Kurt Vonnegut, was an American soldier in Europe in the last year of World War II. If you come to know a combat veteran well—a veteran of that war, of the Korean War, or of the war in Vietnam—you will almost always find that his war experience was the single most important event in his life. The sights and scars of war remain with the soldier for the rest of his days, and his memories of death and killing help to shape whatever future career he may make.

The same is true for Billy Pilgrim. What he saw and did during his six months on the battlefield and as a prisoner of war have dominated his life. *Slaughterhouse-Five* shows how Billy comes to terms with the feelings of horror, guilt, and despair that are the result of his war experiences.

Billy does this by putting the events of his life in perspective. He reorganizes his life so that all of it occurs within the context of his days in Europe during the war. Thus the novel relates Billy's pre-war and postwar history (including his death in 1976, which was many years in the future when Vonnegut was writing this book), but the real story of the novel is the story of Billy's wartime days. All the other events in Billy's life are merely incidental to his time as a soldier and a prisoner of war. You see them as events that come to his mind as he lives, or relives, the last months of the war in Europe.

Billy reorganizes his life by using the device of "time-travel." Unlike everyone else, Billy Pilgrim doesn't live his life one day after another. He has become "unstuck in time," and he jumps around among the periods of his life like a flea from dog to dog.

When you meet him in Chapter 2, it is December 1944 and Billy and three other American soldiers are lost in a forest far behind enemy lines. Billy closes his eyes for a moment, drifts back to a day in his past with his father at the YMCA, then suddenly opens his eyes in the future: it's 1965 and he is visiting his mother in a nursing home. He blinks, the time changes to 1958, then 1961, and then he finds himself back in the forest in December 1944.

Billy doesn't have much time to wonder about what has just happened. He's captured almost immediately by German soldiers and put onto a train bound for eastern Germany. Aboard the train Billy has a great adventure in the future: on his daughter's wedding night in 1967, he is kidnapped by a flying saucer from the imaginary planet Tralfamadore. The aliens take Billy to their home planet and put him in a zoo.

Then, as always seems to happen, Billy wakes up back in the war. The train arrives at a prison camp, and there a group of British officers throw a banquet for the American POWs.

Before long he is traveling in time again, to a mental hospital in 1948, where he's visited by his fiancée, Valencia Merble. As soon as he recovers from his nervous breakdown, Billy will be set up in business as an optometrist by Valencia's father.

Billy is introduced to science fiction by his hospital roommate, Eliot Rosewater, whose favorite author is Kilgore Trout. Trout's writing is terrible, but Billy comes to admire his ideas.

Billy travels in time again to Tralfamadore, where he is the most popular exhibit in the zoo. His keepers love talking to Billy because his ideas are so strange to them. He thinks, for example, that wars could be prevented if people could see into the future as he can.

Next Billy wakes up on the first night of his honeymoon. After making love, Valencia wants to talk about the war. Before Billy can say much about it, he's back there himself.

The American POWs are being moved to Dresden, which as an "open city" (of no military value) has come through the war unscathed, while almost every other German city has been heavily bombed. Billy knows that Dresden will soon be totally destroyed, even though there's nothing worth bombing there—no troops, no weapons factories, nothing but people and beautiful buildings. The Americans are housed in building number five of the Dresden slaughterhouse.

Billy continues his time-travels. He survives a plane crash in 1968. A few years before that, he meets Kilgore Trout. And on Tralfamadore he tells his zoo-mate, Montana Wildhack, about the bombing of Dresden.

Billy Pilgrim and the other American POWs take shelter in a meat locker beneath the slaughterhouse. When they go out the next day, Dresden looks like the surface of the moon. Everything has been reduced to ash and minerals, and everything is still hot. Nothing is moving anywhere.

After months of digging corpses out of the ruins,

Billy and the others wake up one morning to discover that their guards have disappeared. The war is over and they are free.

The Characters

One way to keep straight the many characters in *Slaughterhouse-Five* is to group them according to when they appear in Billy Pilgrim's life.

There are the soldiers he meets during the war (Roland Weary, Paul Lazzaro, Edgar Derby, and Howard W. Campbell, Jr.), the people from his postwar years in Ilium, New York (his wife Valencia, his daughter Barbara, Eliot Rosewater, Kilgore Trout, and Professor Rumfoord), and the characters in his adventure in outer space (the Tralfamadorians and Montana Wildhack).

A fourth group of characters might include the author himself and actual persons in his life, such as Bernard and Mary O'Hare. Some of the characters in this novel had already appeared in earlier novels by Vonnegut: Eliot Rosewater and Kilgore Trout in *God Bless You, Mr. Rosewater*, Howard W. Campbell, Jr., in *Mother Night,* and the Tralfamadorians in *The Sirens of Titan*. Except for the O'Hares, you meet all of these characters only when they interact with Billy Pilgrim.

Billy Pilgrim

Kurt Vonnegut has chosen the names of his characters with care. When you first see a character's name, you usually *know* something about that character even before you read about what he or she has done. Billy Pilgrim's last name tells you that he is someone who travels in foreign lands and that his journeys may have a religious or spiritual aspect.

Otherwise Billy doesn't appear very promising as the hero of a novel. Physically, he's a classic wimp. He's tall, weak, and clumsy, with "a chest and shoulders like a box of kitchen matches" and the overall appearance of "a filthy flamingo."

He has a very passive personality as well. When Billy was a child and his father threw him into a swimming pool, he just went to the bottom and waited to drown. While he is trying to avoid capture by the Germans, three other American soldiers offer him protection and companionship, yet he keeps saying, "You guys go on without me." After the war, he allows himself to be pressured into marrying a stupid and unattractive woman no one else will marry. And he lets his daughter bully him constantly.

In the world of *Slaughterhouse-Five* Billy is a sheep among wolves. Some readers regard him as a kind of Christ figure who sojourns in the wilderness of his past and returns with a message of hope and peace for humanity. They also see a parallel between Billy's assassination by Paul Lazzaro and Jesus' martyrdom on the cross.

But none of the other characters see Billy this way. In the army his "meek faith in a loving Jesus" makes everybody else sick. His pacifism, together with his pathetic attempts to keep warm, make Billy look like a clown in his blue toga and silver shoes.

Although many of the people he meets are thoughtless or cruel to him, the thing that does the most damage to his already fragile personality is the fire-bombing of Dresden. In what kind of world is such a thing possible? Billy is tormented by this question to which he has no answer.

Life seems to victimize Billy at every turn, yet he prefers to turn the other cheek rather than put up a fight. This may be his weakling attempt at "the imitation of Christ," but to many readers it looks a lot like a death wish. But Billy has two things that enable him to survive: a powerful imagination and a belief that at heart people are eager to behave decently. His own belief in goodness never lets him despair, though he comes close to it. Ultimately it's his imagination that saves him.

Before Eliot Rosewater (another disillusioned man) introduces him to science fiction, Billy's fantasies are aimless and childish. Then, in the writings of Kilgore Trout, Billy discovers a kindred spirit who not only agrees that life is crazy but offers alternative versions of reality. This gives Billy the idea of inventing a whole new fantasy world.

In this created world, Billy sees himself as Adam and Montana Wildhack as Eve. In order for this brave new world to work, Billy must become "innocent" again, and to do this he has to discharge the guilt and despair associated with his past. He does this by reorganizing his life through time-travel, gradually putting everything—but especially Dresden—in perspective. When this is accomplished, his pilgrimage is over and Billy is free.

Roland Weary

A soldier in combat is always on duty, his life constantly at risk, the tension sometimes unbearable. You know when you first see his name that Billy's fellow soldier Roland Weary is exhausted after many months of fighting. What he needs is some rest.

Weary is a hard person to like: he's stupid, fat, and mean, and he smells bad. It's no surprise that his companions want to "ditch" him most of the time. So Weary has had to learn to deal with rejection, and one way he does this is by fantasizing a glorious and exciting war movie in which he is the hero. Because Weary fears that his real-life companions, the army scouts, will abandon him, his war movie concentrates on the deep, manly friendships he wishes he had in real life.

Weary knows that the scouts will try to get rid of him sooner or later. His "Three Musketeers" story is only a fantasy. He will want revenge when he is ditched, and he usually gets his revenge by ditching someone else. So he picks up a poor misfit who is even less popular than himself, suckers him into a friendship, then ditches him first. This time his would-be victim is Billy Pilgrim.

One nice thing happens to Roland Weary. He gets to die in the way he would have wanted—in the arms of a true friend, Paul Lazzaro. Weary has finally found a kindred spirit, and he can rest at last, knowing that Lazzaro intends to carry out the last mission of Weary's life, to kill Billy Pilgrim.

Paul Lazzaro
The American POW Paul Lazzaro is the ugliest and meanest character in the book. Not only is he disgusting to look at, he's nasty to the core, a real snake. In civilian life his friends are gangsters and killers, and he may be a gangster himself. The sweetest thing in life to him is getting revenge on people who have crossed him.

It's not surprising that he and Roland Weary become buddies. Both of them have regularly been snubbed by the more popular and attractive people in their lives. Yet Lazzaro is more pure in his ugliness than Weary. When Weary rambles on about different kinds of torture, he's speaking in the abstract, not talking about torturing anyone in particular. But when Lazzaro dreams up ways of hurting people, each torture is tailor-made for a specific victim.

Vonnegut's description of Lazzaro is devastating: "If he had been a dog in a city, a policeman would have shot him and sent his head to a laboratory, to see if he had rabies."

Edgar Derby

At the time of World War II, men and boys everywhere still wore hats whenever they went outdoors. But by then the derby, a hat with a dome-shaped crown, had become a bit out of date and was usually seen only on older men. Thus, you can tell by his name that Edgar Derby is an older man than his fellow American POWs, and his values are those he learned in an earlier era.

Because you know from the first that "poor old Edgar Derby" (as he is usually called) is doomed, you watch his gentle acts of kindness and generosity with a sinking heart. For Edgar Derby doesn't deserve to die. It is Derby who cradles the dying Weary's head in his lap (whatever Paul Lazzaro says), and it is Derby who volunteers to sit in the prison hospital with a crazed and doped-up Billy Pilgrim while the other Americans party with the Englishmen.

Derby believes that World War II is a just war. He had even pulled strings to get into the fighting after the army told him he was too old. And in Dresden, when the American Nazi Howard W. Campbell, Jr., tries to talk the prisoners into going over to his side, Derby stands up to him and makes a moving speech about the ideals of America: "freedom and justice and opportunities and fair play for all." This takes courage, considering the position he's in.

Valencia Merble Pilgrim

Billy first checks into the mental hospital after hearing himself propose marriage to this over-weight, not very bright daughter of Ilium's richest optometrist. He sees her as "a symptom of his disease," his inability to deal with the alarming reality of the world and his lack of interest in life. But he marries her anyway, apparently for lack of a good reason not to. The marriage is hardly a great romance, but Billy finds it "at least bearable all the way." His unhappiness seems to have less to do with her than with life itself.

Considering that Vonnegut frequently prefers female over male values, it's difficult to find much to admire in Valencia. Not only is she unattractive, she's insensitive to the deep psychological damage Billy underwent in the war, from which he continues to suffer.

But for all her faults, Valencia adores Billy and is helplessly devoted to him. She is so terrified of losing him after he barely survives a plane crash that she wrecks her car on the way to the hospital, passes out, and dies from carbon monoxide fumes.

Barbara Pilgrim

Barbara Pilgrim, Billy's put-upon daughter, has hardly had a chance to get married and set up her own household when her father almost dies in a plane crash. While he is in the hospital, her mother inadvertently kills herself in an auto accident. Then, when Billy comes home, he turns out to be prematurely senile from brain damage and begins telling crazy stories about time-travel and aliens kidnapping him in a flying saucer. Not only is she suddenly the head of the family, but her father's making a laughing stock of himself (and her) in public.

No wonder Barbara's a "bitchy flibbertigibbet."

Bertram Copeland Rumfoord

Billy meets Rumfoord while recuperating from the plane crash in 1968. Relentlessly virile and athletic, this seventy-year-old Harvard professor and Air Force historian embodies every traditional "masculine virtue" Billy finds so upsetting: blind patriotism, sexism (his young fifth wife is just "one more public demonstration" that he's a "superman"), and a firm belief in the survival of the fittest.

Vonnegut uses Rumfoord as the primary spokesman for what he calls the "military manner" of thinking, which orders and then cravenly justifies atrocities such as the bombing of Dresden.

The Tralfamadorians

The Tralfamadorians are "two feet high, and green, and shaped like plumber's friends" topped by "a little hand with a green eye in its palm." They can see in four dimensions, and this enables them to look at all time all at once, so death and the future hold no fear for them. The Tralfamadorians, who

live on a distant planet, are creatures of science
fiction.

Because of their alien perspective, the Tralfamadorians view human behavior with an objectiv-
ity few Earthlings can have. In this way, Vonnegut
may be using the Tralfamadorians to tell you what
he thinks about human conduct. Whenever the
Tralfamadorians speak, Vonnegut may be reveal-
ing his own philosophy of life.

Some readers argue that the purpose of the Tralfamadorians is to resolve the contradictions in life
that have made Billy so upset. In this interpretation, the aliens function in the same way as dreams
and mythology: they "explain" things through images and stories.

Others see the Tralfamadorians as the "gods" in
Billy's fantasy universe: they guide and protect the
creatures in their charge. This makes them a big
improvement over the "gods" Vonnegut sees as
the rulers of the modern world—technology, which
dehumanizes people, and authoritarian cruelty,
which destroys people in the name of the "survival
of the fittest."

The Tralfamadorians give Billy a philosophy
through which he finds peace of mind. They also
give him Montana Wildhack to mate with, and that
brings him true happiness as well.

Montana Wildhack

Billy's lover in this alien zoo is a curious combi-
nation of ingredients. On the one hand, she is the
compliant sex kitten that bored, middle-aged males
dream about in erotic fantasies. She is beautiful
(and naked), and makes the first sexual ad-
vances—though shyly, of course.

On the other hand, Billy requires more from his dream woman than mere sexuality. His entire Tralfamadore fantasy is his attempt to reinvent the human race, with himself as the new Adam and Montana as the new Eve. And so he makes her loving as well as sexy, understanding as well as seductive, and a good mother to their child as well as a good lover to him. In Billy's ideal Creation, both must be able to behave as decently as he believes Adam and Eve really wanted to behave.

For all of her prodigious virtues, Montana Wildhack comes off as rather bloodless compared to the real-life women in the book, such as the annoying Valencia, the prickly Barbara, or the fiery Mary O'Hare. But then Billy prefers fantasy to real life. It's a lot safer.

Eliot Rosewater

One of the richest and smartest men in America, Eliot Rosewater is also one of the most disillusioned. His faith in American righteousness in World War II was shattered when he found that he had killed a German fireman who was trying to put out a fire that American bombers had started.

He tried drinking, but that just ruined his health without alleviating what he saw as the alarming unfairness of the modern world. So he committed himself to a mental hospital. There he meets a kindred spirit in Billy Pilgrim, who comes to share with him the one consolation Eliot has found in life: the peculiar wisdom in the science fiction of Kilgore Trout.

Kilgore Trout

The science fiction writer Kilgore Trout has great ideas for novels. (*The Gutless Wonder* is about a ro-

bot with bad breath; in *The Gospel from Outer Space*
Jesus is a nobody until God adopts him.) But his
prose style is frightful. After thirty years and more
than seventy-five novels, Trout has only two fans,
Eliot Rosewater and Billy Pilgrim, and even they
are appalled by his writing.

Kilgore Trout is a manic version of Kurt Vonnegut, who also wrote science fiction and for years
suffered from an indifferent public. Vonnegut uses
Trout's books to make fun of many of the values
Americans hold dear. At the same time, he gets in
a few good swipes at the pretensions of his own
profession.

In *Slaughterhouse-Five* (as in the two other Vonnegut novels in which he appears) Kilgore Trout
plays a small but important role. His books offer
Billy inspiration for therapeutic fantasies, and he
personally gives Billy the courage to face his Dresden experience.

Howard W. Campbell, Jr.

Campbell is an American Nazi propagandist who
writes a scornful account of the behavior of American POWs in Germany and who shows up at the
slaughterhouse in Dresden to recruit candidates
for his Free American Corps. He tries to bribe the
Americans by promising them a terrific meal, but
Edgar Derby puts Campbell in his place by calling
him "lower . . . than a blood-filled tick." Campbell
only smiles.

In an earlier book, *Mother Night*, Vonnegut told
Campbell's whole story—he's really an American
spy who delivers coded messages to the Allies
through his racist radio broadcasts. But in *Slaugh-*

terhouse we see him only in his "official" role as the Nazi he pretends to be.

Mary O'Hare

Vonnegut dedicates this book to a real person, Mary O'Hare, the wife of his old war buddy Bernard V. O'Hare. He first meets her when he tries to get Bernard to reminisce with him about their war experiences, with the idea of generating material for his "famous book about Dresden." This makes Mary angry. She cares deeply about life—she's a nurse—and to her, all war does is kill people. She is strong-minded and courageous enough to tell off an almost perfect stranger when she thinks he's wrong.

Vonnegut admires Mary O'Hare and wishes more people were like her. He believes that if enough women like her told off enough "old farts" like him, enough people might see the absurdity of war and we wouldn't have wars any more.

Bernard V. O'Hare

When Vonnegut visits Bernard O'Hare after the war, O'Hare appears to be little more than a henpecked husband, and acts embarrassed when Vonnegut tries to get him reminiscing about the war.

But O'Hare had refused to pick up souvenirs in Dresden, so even then he must have hated the war and the "profit" some people made from it (his buddies with their "trophies," Vonnegut with his book). He's a gentle man who reproaches no one: when Vonnegut asks why Mary is mad, O'Hare lies to spare Vonnegut's feelings. And even though he disapproves of Vonnegut's project, he is kind enough to leave a book about Dresden on the nightstand for him.

O'Hare is a great friend, and Vonnegut obviously likes him a lot. He's the only war buddy Vonnegut has kept in touch with, and together they return to Dresden in 1967.

Kurt Vonnegut

The author himself appears in *Slaughterhouse-Five*, mainly in the first chapter, where he struggles vainly to get a handle on writing his Dresden book. His breakthrough comes when Mary O'Hare reminds him that it's really babies who fight wars, not grown men. From that moment on everything goes right for the author.

Vonnegut also pops up here and there in Billy Pilgrim's POW story, but he's really just reminding you that what those American prisoners of war saw and did really happened—and that he was there at the time. In the last chapter he tells about his return to Dresden as a tourist in 1967 with Bernard O'Hare.

Other Elements
SETTING

There are three main settings in *Slaughterhouse-Five*.

1. War-ravaged Europe, through which Billy travels as a POW and ends up in Dresden.

2. Peacetime America, where Billy prospers as an optometrist and pillar of society in Ilium, New York.

3. The planet Tralfamadore, where Billy and

his fantasy lover Montana Wildhack are exhibited in a zoo.

Each setting corresponds to a different period in Billy Pilgrim's life, and the story jumps from one setting to another as Billy travels back and forth in time.

The physical contrast between the devastation of Europe and the affluence of postwar America is tremendous. It's ironic that Billy, who suffered extreme privations as a prisoner of war, is made to feel no better by the material wealth he later acquires as a successful optometrist in Ilium, N.Y.

Ilium is the classical name for Troy, one of the richest cities in the ancient world. In *The Iliad*, the Greek poet Homer (ninth century B.C.) tells the story of the Trojan War, in which Troy was eventually destroyed by the besieging Greeks. Some readers believe that *Slaughterhouse-Five* is Kurt Vonnegut's *Iliad*, for Troy was reputedly as beautiful as Dresden was before it was bombed.

Billy begins to be happy about life only in an artificial but cozy habitat on another planet. Tralfamadore is an invention of Billy's imagination, a paradise in which he, as Adam, and a new Eve (the former pornographic movie star Montana Wildhack) can start the human race over again. Within the dome that protects them from the poisonous atmosphere of Tralfamadore, Billy and Montana are tended and watched over by a new set of gods, the wise and kindly Tralfamadorians.

But notice that in each of the novel's main settings Billy is confined: first as a POW, then as a prisoner of the meaningless contraptions of modern life, finally as an exhibit in an alien zoo. And throughout the book Vonnegut portrays Billy as a prisoner of time. Billy cannot change the past, the present, or the future, no matter how much he moves around from one to the other. The persistent image of a bug trapped in amber is Vonnegut's clearest expression of this idea.

THEMES

Slaughterhouse-Five is first and foremost about war and how human beings cope with it. In treating this subject, Vonnegut explores several major themes, but no single one of them explains the whole novel. You'll find that some of the following statements ring more true to you than others, yet you can find evidence in the book to support all of them.

War Is Absurd

Vonnegut attacks the reasoning that leads people to commit atrocities by drawing character portraits (Roland Weary and Professor Rumfoord) and by quoting from official documents (President Harry Truman's explanation of the reasons for dropping the atomic bomb on Hiroshima). And he gives you a look at the ruins of Dresden so you can see the "ground zero" consequences of what he calls the military manner of thinking—which rationalizes a massacre by saying it will hasten the end of the war.

But more important than this generalized condemnation, Vonnegut focuses on the enormity of war and its disastrous effect on human lives, even long after it is over. Billy Pilgrim's problems all stem from what he experienced in the war. The hobo freezes to death in the boxcar; Roland Weary dies from gangrene in his feet; Edgar Derby is shot for stealing a teapot; the harmless city of Dresden is bombed into the ground: it shouldn't be possible for such things to happen, Billy feels. And yet he was there and saw them happen with his own eyes. His science fiction fantasies and time-traveling are his attempt to cope with the psychological damage the war inflicted on him. The fact that he succeeds (by going senile) is perhaps the most absurd thing of all.

Authority Is to Blame for Atrocities

To Vonnegut, both the boss and the underling escape guilt when an atrocity is committed: the boss's hands are clean because others did the dirty work, and the underling was only following orders. He maintains that this was just as true of the Allies as it was of the Nazis in World War II. The Nazis built the death camps, and the Allies bombed Hiroshima and Dresden.

Vonnegut believes that a great evil of authoritarianism is the assumption of righteousness, the claim that "God is on our side." In other writings he expresses regret that the Nazis were so plainly evil because that just made it easier for the Allied authorities to claim that anything they did to defeat the Nazis was justified.

To Vonnegut this is the same kind of authoritarian arrogance that led the Nazis into evil acts in the first place. There is no moral justification for atrocities, Vonnegut says, even though some defenders of the Dresden bombing maintain that it did accomplish its goal: to end the war sooner by demoralizing the enemy.

Modern Life Is Meaningless
Billy Pilgrim's indifference to life comes as much from his peacetime experiences as from anything that happened to him in the war. During the war he could at least tell whether he was alive or dead. But his postwar life is empty in spite of his material wealth and the respect of his peers.

Vonnegut highlights this apparent contradiction by having Billy find peace and happiness only through fantasy (or senility). Vonnegut seems to say that in real life, life doesn't work.

Art vs. Reality
Vonnegut spends a good deal of time in *Slaughterhouse-Five* talking about fiction. In Chapter 1 he shows how a writer distorts reality by forcing it to fit into the mold of a "good story." In Chapter 5 he discusses the good and bad effects fiction has on our understanding of life. In Chapter 9 he pokes fun at the pretensions of writers and critics who take fiction too seriously. And the "fragmented style" in which *Slaughterhouse-Five* is written may be an attempt to reinvent the novel. As Eliot Rosewater says, fiction just "isn't *enough* any more."

Part of the difficulty lies in the nature of art itself. Art selects and orders its material, and the final product is a coherent whole. But life is messy and redundant: it can't be contained in the neat formula of a story with a beginning, a middle, and an end. In the case of such a horrifying event as the Dresden massacre, art has nothing intelligent to say.

Some readers believe that Vonnegut overstates the problem in *Slaughterhouse-Five*, that the book itself is the solution. Just as Billy Pilgrim reinvents

his life so he can cope with it, Vonnegut reinvents
the novel so that it can cope with the absurd and
often monstrous events of the modern world.

Technology Dehumanizes People

Machine imagery abounds in *Slaughterhouse-Five*,
and wherever it turns up, it means bad news for
human beings. Obviously, without sophisticated
technology, the atomic bomb that devastated Hiroshima would not have been possible. But Vonnegut portrays even peacetime technology as making people into robots whose lives revolve around
tending and improving machines. Billy's father-in-
law, Lionel Merble, for example, is turned into a
machine by the optometry business.

There are several additional themes that Vonnegut only touches on in *Slaughterhouse-Five*, but
which are given fuller treatment in his other books.

Free Will vs. Determinism

At first the heroes of almost all Vonnegut's novels
believe in free will. (Free will is the idea that human beings make choices and decide their own
destinies, that their actions make a difference in
shaping their futures.) But inevitably Vonnegut's
heroes discover that their choices were manipu-
lated by outside forces, that their fates were pre-
determined all along. Billy Pilgrim is Vonnegut's
most passive hero. He finds happiness and peace
of mind only after adopting the deterministic philosophy of his imaginary masters, the Tralfamadorians.

Darwin vs. Jesus

Vonnegut feels that Charles Darwin legitimized
cruelty with his theory of natural selection. Al-

though Darwin limited his theorizing to biology, other thinkers like the English philosopher Herbert Spencer (1820–1903) applied this theory to social matters, and took Darwin's idea that the strong are favored in natural survival one step further, implying that only the strong *should* survive. It is this version of "social" Darwinism that Vonnegut disapproves of. In contrast, although he has been an atheist all his life, Vonnegut has always admired the Christian virtues of pacifism, tolerance, and love.

Organized Religion

Vonnegut doesn't have much good will toward organized religion. For him it is no different from any other form of authority, and therefore it is capable of the same or greater evils. How many atrocities have been justified by the claim that "God is on our side"?

Death

People are dying constantly in *Slaughterhouse-Five*, and of course the destruction of Dresden brought death on a massive scale. Vonnegut follows every mention of death with that familiar phrase, "So it goes." In this way he attempts to find a saner attitude toward death by emphasizing that death is a common aspect of human existence. Billy Pilgrim finds consolation in the Tralfamadorian notion that people who are dead in the present remain alive in the times of their past. Perhaps the author is saying that we too should be consoled: the dead still live in our memories.

STYLE

On the second page of Chapter 5, a Tralfamadorian explains the nature of novels on that planet:

> "Each clump of symbols is a brief, urgent mes-
> sage—describing a situation, a scene. We Tral-
> famadorians read them all at once, not one after
> the other. There isn't any particular relation-
> ship between all the messages, except that the
> author has chosen them carefully, so that, when
> seen all at once, they produce an image of life
> that is beautiful and surprising and deep. There
> is no beginning, no middle, no end, no sus-
> pense, no moral, no causes, no effects. What
> we love in our books are the depths of many
> marvelous moments seen all at one time."

When you come upon this passage in the novel,
you may feel a shock of recognition. It sounds a
lot like the very book you're reading, and you realize that the author is describing the effect he wants
his novel to have.

The most striking aspect of the style of *Slaughterhouse-Five* is the fact that the text is made up of
clumps of paragraphs, each clump set off by extra
space before and after it. A few of the clumps are
only one sentence long. Some are as long as a page
and a half. Each of them makes a simple statement
or relates an incident or situation. Thus the novel
is said to be written in an *anecdotal* style: the book
is a collection of brief incidents, and the effect of
each one depends on how the author tells it.

Vonnegut generally uses short, simple sen-
tences that manage to say a great deal in a few
words. "Three inoffensive *bangs* came from far
away." The report seems an innocent one until
you find out that the scouts have just been shot.

The contrast between the "inoffensive" sound and its deadly meaning provides a startling effect.

There is irony too in that "inoffensive," for what is inoffensive to one person's ears is fatally offensive to another person's life. Irony is a form of humor that occurs when a seemingly straightforward statement or situation actually means its opposite. Irony occurs again and again in the incidents Vonnegut describes. It is ironic that, for all that the Bible represents as a statment of ethics, a soldier carries a bullet-proof Bible sheathed in steel. There is irony in a former hobo's telling Billy—inside a boxcar prison that could be taking them to their death—"I been in worse places than this. This ain't so bad." And because Dresden was an "open city" during most of the war, it was full of refugees who had fled there for safety. Almost all of them died in the bombing. That is ironic.

Another kind of humor that the author relies on heavily is satire, a form of ridicule that uses mockery and exaggeration to expose the foolishness or evil of its subject. Professor Rumfoord is a satirical portrait of the all-American male ideal. And, almost every description of a Kilgore Trout novel satirizes modern life in some way. A killer robot becomes popular only after his bad breath is cleared up (advertising values), or a money tree is fertilized by the dead bodies of those who killed each other to get its "fruit" (material values).

Vonnegut has a powerful gift for tangy imagery. He describes Billy as a filthy flamingo and a broken kite, the Russian prisoner as "a ragbag with a round, flat face that glowed like a radium dial."

Sometimes his images border on the tasteless: an antitank gun makes "a ripping sound like the

opening of the zipper on the fly of God Almighty."
But Vonnegut also creates images of almost heart-
breaking tenderness, as in the picture of Edgar
Derby bursting into tears when Billy feeds him a
spoonful of malt syrup.

Vonnegut layers his storytelling with allusions
(references) to historical events. He evokes the
Children's Crusade in order to draw a parallel between the "babies" he and O'Hare were in World
War II and the thirteenth-century religious expe-
dition in which European children were sent off to
conquer the Holy Land. He refers to works of literature: the novels of the French Nazi sympathizer
Céline, the medieval heroic epic poem *The Song of
Roland*, and the Bible. He paraphrases the Sodom
and Gomorrah story from Genesis and mentions
Jesus occasionally. These allusions deepen our understanding and appreciation of Billy's story by
suggesting historical and literary parallels to the
personal events in his life.

POINT OF VIEW

In Chapter 1 (and in portions of Chapter 10) the
author speaks to you directly in the first person
about the difficult time he had writing his book.
The rest of the book is Billy Pilgrim's story told by
a third-person narrator.

Because an outside narrator is telling Billy's story,
you learn not only what Billy is doing and thinking
at any time but what the other characters are up
to and what's on their minds. Because Vonnegut
explains, in his first-person appearances as the
writer-narrator, that his own experiences in Dresden were the inspiration for *Slaughterhouse-Five*,

many readers assume that both the third-person narrator and Billy Pilgrim represent the author. In this view, the author is looking at the events of his own life—past, present, and future—and trying to make some sense out of them the same way that Billy is trying to order the events of his own life.

On several occasions the author actually reminds you directly that, while he's telling Billy's story, he—Kurt Vonnegut—was there, too. You're reading about events that are based on the author's experience as a POW in Dresden. These interruptions also warn you that you're being told a story by a much older man, someone with a quite different outlook on life from that of the "baby" who went to Dresden.

The flexible perspective of the narration allows Vonnegut to comment frequently on the action, on life, and on writing itself.

FORM AND STRUCTURE

As explained in Chapter 5 of *Slaughterhouse-Five,* Tralfamadorians read the clumps of symbols, or messages, that make up their books all at once. But human beings must read the clumps of paragraphs that make up *Slaughterhouse-Five* one by one, and the order in which the author has set them out for you provides the structure of the novel.

Vonnegut starts with a chapter of introduction or prologue in which he tells his own story of writing his "famous book about Dresden."

The rest of the book, Chapters 2 through 10, tells Billy Pilgrim's story. Vonnegut begins this narrative with a short, factual history of Billy's life to the present in 1968. You soon discover why he does this: in the pages that follow, Billy's adventures are not related entirely in chronological order, and that little outline history in the early pages of Chapter 2 lets you read on without having to puzzle over the proper sequence of events.

The portion of Billy Pilgrim's history that is presented chronologically is the six months from December 1944 to May 1945, when Billy was a soldier and then a POW in Europe. This period is by far the most important in Billy's life, and the novel is about how Billy comes to terms with what he saw and heard and did in those six months. When Billy finally works it all out in his mind, he is free, the author has finished his Dresden book, and the novel has ended.

Therefore the basic structure of *Slaughterhouse-Five* is determined by the sequence of events Billy experienced in the final months of World War II. Into this sequence Billy fits all the other happenings of his life. He even believes that he first "came unstuck in time" in the Luxembourg forest in 1944, though the narrator seems to suggest that this weird phenomenon was actually the result of the brain damage Billy sustained in the plane crash in 1968.

Because Billy is reinventing his life by reorganizing his memories and adding his fantasies, it's important that you keep your bearings as you follow Billy's own rearrangement of his history. For this you may find helpful the following chronological sequence of the important events in Billy's life.

1922	Billy born in Ilium, New York.
1941	America enters World War II.

1944	Billy, now a soldier, captured by Germans in the Battle of the Bulge. He spends Christmas on a POW train headed for Czechoslovakia.
1945 January	Billy arrives in Dresden, is put to work in a factory, is housed in Slaughterhouse-Five.
1945 February	Dresden fire-bombed by the Allies. POWs and guards survive in an underground locker and begin to dig bodies out of the rubble the next day.
1945 May	War ends in Europe and POWs are released. Billy goes home to Ilium.
1948	Billy recovers from a nervous breakdown, marries Valencia Merble, fathers Robert and Barbara. The optometry business in Ilium prospers.
1967	Barbara marries. Billy kidnapped the same night and taken to Tralfamadore, where he is exhibited in a zoo and mated with Montana Wildhack.
1968	Billy survives plane crash in Vermont. Valencia dies while Billy is recovering. Billy goes to New York City to tell about the Tralfamadorians.
1976	Billy assassinated in Chicago after speaking on flying saucers and time.

The Story

Vonnegut's method of storytelling sometimes makes it difficult to follow him or to see his point in a welter of apparently unrelated anecdotes. To help you along, the discussion of each chapter in this section begins with a brief overview of the chapter's structure.

CHAPTER 1

Structure: The string of anecdotes that lead up to Vonnegut's visit with the O'Hares all describe problems related to writing his "famous book about Dresden." After his visit to the O'Hares, things start going well for him, and he is able to write the book. In the last part of the chapter Vonnegut finds solutions to (or at least ways around) his writing problems.

Let's look at some of those problems the author complains about.

The words just won't come. Although he thought it would be easy to write about Dresden—"all I would have to do would be to report what I had seen"—he just can't seem to get started. Vonnegut may be afraid that he has used up his talent, or somehow ruined it (the off-color limerick suggests this idea), perhaps by writing so much science fiction instead of "saving himself" for his "great book about Dresden."

Every time he starts the book, he ends up going in circles. The Yon Yonson poem illustrates this dilemma. Once you start it, you go around and around forever.

Another antiwar book would be pointless. This problem is clearly stated in the conversation Vonnegut has with the movie director. Books don't stop wars because wars are as unstoppable as glaciers are.

Writing isn't the noble profession everyone thinks it is. Vonnegut calls himself a "trafficker in climaxes and thrills and characterization and wonderful dialogue and suspense and confrontations." He goes on to describe a diagram he made that reduces every human being to a line of color and makes the destruction of Dresden nothing but a brilliant stripe of orange. What was once an atrocity has now become something abstract and "pretty."

NOTE: Parallel Images   This chapter is full of images that resurface in altered form later in the book. In Chapter 4, for example, the Tralfamadorians use the metaphor of bugs trapped in amber to describe human beings caught in time. This image parallels the idea of characters "trapped" in a diagram for a story. The "idiotic Englishman" with his absurd souvenir turns up again in the guise of Roland Weary displaying his weapons to Billy (Chapter 2) and later (Chapter 6) as Billy himself, showing his "treasures" to the Dresden surgeon. In a way the Englishman is also like Vonnegut trying to interest O'Hare in his Dresden story. Vonnegut is not only struggling with writing problems here, he is generating material that he will rework into Billy's story.

Writing won't help Vonnegut find meaning in his life. Vonnegut isn't very happy with himself. He's getting old, he's killing himself with alcohol and cigarettes, he and his wife don't communicate any more. Maybe life itself is a rut he fell into: before he knew it he's "an old fart with his memories and his Pall Malls."

Writing dehumanizes the writer. The gruesome story of the veteran's being killed by an elevator points up this problem. Nancy does to the veteran the same thing that Vonnegut wants to do with Edgar Derby—she dehumanizes him by making him a character in a story. This in turn dehumanizes her, making her unable to feel anything for the suffering of others. Vonnegut fears that even if he does finish his Dresden book, the very act of constructing a good story will turn him into a callous creep.

NOTE: Machine Imagery   One of Vonnegut's favorite themes is the uneasy relationship between man and machines, and this anecdote is shot through with machine imagery. It's even possible to see the News Bureau as being run by its machines. And it's ironic that the veteran is killed by getting his hand caught in an iron gate that is imitating life forms—iron ivy, iron twigs, iron lovebirds. Keep an eye out for other instances of such imagery.

What can you say about a massacre? The cocktail party anecdote, where Vonnegut hears about the death camps, illustrates another problem. How do you respond when someone tells you these ghastly stories? "Oh, my *God*" doesn't say very much, does it? That's Vonnegut's point.

These problems frustrated Vonnegut for twenty-three years, until he visited the O'Hares. You should look at this anecdote in some detail. He begins by describing the trip from Cape Cod as seen through the eyes of two little girls, his daughter and her friend. To them the world is full of strange sights, including rivers and waterfalls to stop and wonder at. The peaceful scene contrasts sharply with the purpose of the trip, which is to reminisce about the war—as if that time of destruction and death were "the good old days."

O'Hare is embarrassed about reminiscing, and his wife Mary seems intent on keeping him that way. She bangs ice trays, moves furniture, and mutters to herself. When she finally tells Vonnegut off, he too is embarrassed because he realizes he's been thinking and acting like a fool about his "famous book on Dresden."

NOTE: Embarrassment   Doesn't every anecdote in this chapter deal with embarrassment? Vonnegut has consistently portrayed himself as a fool: a grown man playing with crayons, an "idiotic Englishman" with his stupid souvenir, an "old fart" who talks to his dog, a green reporter trying to act tough. The point is that he doesn't realize how embarrassing his actions have been until he encounters Mary O'Hare. Perhaps Vonnegut is saying that embarrassment, not horror, is the proper way to feel about atrocities committed in war. It is those people who are not embarrassed who are dangerous. They are the ones who come up with the kind of thinking that says, "We have to bomb Dresden so we can end the war sooner."

Vonnegut also has a tangible breakthrough while

visiting the O'Hares: he conceives the idea of calling his book "The Children's Crusade." Coming
up with a title may help a writer to crystallize his
thinking on a subject or get him going in the right
direction. This seems to happen to Vonnegut.

NOTE: The Crusades   There were approximately
seven Crusades between the years 1095 and 1271.
The Christian powers of Europe sent these military
expeditions to Palestine in a mostly unsuccessful
attempt to regain possession of the Holy Land from
the Moslems. The name *crusade* comes from the
Latin word *crux*, meaning cross. Vonnegut's description of the Children's Crusade is pretty ac-
curate.

Note how Vonnegut puts together two ideas that
ought to be totally contradictory: holy and war.
The book is full of such ironic juxtapositions, so
keep an eye out for them.

The senselessness of the historical Children's
Crusade provides Vonnegut with a parallel to the
destruction of Dresden. And he learns that Dresden had been bombed before, just as pointlessly.
The quote from the great German poet, Johann
Wolfgang von Goethe (1749–1832) conveys Vonnegut's view. The caretaker of the Frauenkirche
(Church of Our Lady) is showing the undamaged
dome to his young visitor. This is what our great
architect did, he tells Goethe. Then he gestures at
the bombed-out ruins around the church and says,
that is what the enemy did!
Vonnegut's visit to the O'Hares has been fruit-

ful, and on the way home he finds additional material. At the New York World's Fair he and the girls see "official versions" of the past and future that make him wonder about the present: "how wide it was, how deep it was, how much was mine to keep." This suggests one of the major subjects of the book, the nature of time and how it works.

Suddenly Vonnegut is asked to teach in one of the most prestigious writing programs in the country. And he gets a three-book contract. Nothing had worked before, but everything is working now. He finishes the book.

NOTE: Vonnegut's self-deprecation   Vonnegut often mocks himself and his writing. Some readers see this as false modesty, others believe he's sincere. *Slaughterhouse-Five* has a lot of intelligent things to say about the destruction of Dresden—about the thinking that caused it, about the effect it had on the people who survived it, about what he sees as the right way and the wrong way to remember it. The book is *not* a failure, for it made Vonnegut's reputation and is generally considered his masterpiece. And *Slaughterhouse-Five* informed the public that Dresden—at least in terms of number of people killed—was the worst single bombing attack of the war.

Before concluding his account of the writing of *Slaughterhouse-Five*, Vonnegut takes us back to Dresden in 1967. (You remember he mentioned this trip at the beginning of the chapter.) Underneath the rebuilt Dresden, where Vonnegut and

O'Hare are having so much fun, "there must be tons of human bone meal in the ground." Bone meal is a fertilizer made from grinding up the bones of slaughterhouse animals. The present Dresden sprang up like a flower from the sterile ground of "the moon" (what Dresden looked like after it was bombed), aided by the fertilizer of crushed human bones.

NOTE: Resonance   This image, like so many others in *Slaughterhouse-Five*, has an extraordinary resonance. In music, resonance is the enrichment of sound by means of echoes. If you've ever been in a large church when the choir is singing, you know how rich that sound can be: the voices bounce off the walls and increase the vibration in the air. In literature, an image is resonant when it reminds us of other images and enriches our understanding by connecting things that didn't seem related before.

The final anecdote in Chapter 1, Vonnegut's "non-night" in Boston, shows him "locking in" on the main ideas that *Slaughterhouse-Five* will embody. The first idea he presents has to do with the difference between time as we think of it and time as we experience it. Remember the scene where Vonnegut and the two girls stood looking at the Hudson River? This is our image of external time: it flows at a steady rate in one direction, from the past through the present toward the future. But in our minds we can jump from the past (memory) to the future (fantasy or planning) without having to go through the "time" in between. We can also go backward as well as forward in time. And not only can it feel as though it takes a year for a second to pass, but a lifetime can seem as though it's over in a second. Vonnegut may be suggesting that this internal time is more real to us than the external time of clocks and calendars.

Vonnegut explores this idea in the quotations from the French writer Louis-Ferdinand Céline, which say that the passage of time leads inevitably to death, and if time could be stopped, no one would die. We know that the flow of external time cannot be stopped. But internal time is a different matter. Don't we do exactly what Céline wants to do—stop people from disappearing—in our memories? And isn't that what Vonnegut does with Dresden in writing *Slaughterhouse-Five*?

NOTE: The novelist Louis-Ferdinand Céline (1894–1961) had a reputation in France equal to that of Ernest Hemingway in America. But in the late 1930s Céline declared himself to be an antisemite and a Nazi sympathizer, and after World War II was tried and imprisoned as a war criminal. It seems amazing, but Vonnegut claims that Céline had a great influence on him. In an essay published in 1974, he explains what Céline meant to him and why he admires him so much. He is willing to forgive what he calls Céline's "racism and cracked politics" because he was a great and inspiring writer: ". . . in my opinion, Céline gave us in his novels the finest history we have of the total collapse of Western civilization in two world wars, as witnessed by hideously vulnerable common women and men."

Another idea that Vonnegut is fond of can be found in the American poet Theodore Roethke's poem, which implies that we are not masters of our destinies, as we like to imagine, but that we get the hang of life by doing what circumstances force us to do.

NOTE: Man as victim/agent   Howard W. Campbell, Jr., the American Nazi whom we will meet later, is a perfect example of this theme. In *Mother Night* he's an American spy whose radio broadcasts contain coded messages about Nazi troop movements and battle plans. After the war he is tried as a war criminal because of the obvious damage he did as a Nazi propagandist. Whether he was a real Nazi or just pretending to be one makes no difference.

Another idea presented in this anecdote comes from the biblical Sodom and Gomorrah story, an example of the kind of "good story" Vonnegut doesn't want his Dresden book to be. Sodom and Gomorrah are destroyed because they are evil. Lot and his family are spared because they are good. But there's a wrinkle in this otherwise typical "tale of great destruction": Lot's wife looks back and is turned into a pillar of salt.

This is a particularly rich image. In the first place, she might never have thought of looking back until she was told not to. (You know the feeling of wanting something only after you've been told you can't have it.) But Vonnegut hints at another reason she might have had: "Lot's wife, of course, was told not to look back where all those people and their homes had been. But she *did* look back, and I love her for that, because she was so human."

Does this remind you of Mary O'Hare? Vonnegut often gives the values he admires most to the women characters in his books, implying that women are more humane than men. Some see Vonnegut's preference for women's values as a subtle form of male chauvinism. According to this interpretation, the tough reporter Nancy lost her humanity by taking a man's job, while Mary O'Hare retained hers by staying home with the babies. Vonnegut seems to support this argument when he says, "The very toughest reporters and writers were women who had taken over the jobs of men who'd gone to war." On the other hand, the war made it necessary for women to leave home and go to work—and men started the war.

NOTE: *Lysistrata*   In the literature of ancient Greece a very funny play by Aristophanes, *Lysistrata*, offers an ingenious solution to the problem of war. In the play, Athens and Sparta have been at war for twenty years, and the women are fed up. So they go on a "sex strike," demanding that the men sign a peace treaty. After a while the men become so desperate they have to agree. (In real life the war dragged on for seven more years and ended only when Athens was destroyed.)

Even if you think that Vonnegut is a "closet male chauvinist," others say that his main point is not that a woman's place is in the home but that a *human being's* place is not in a war.

CHAPTER 2

Structure: In this chapter you meet Billy Pilgrim and get a taste of his peculiar experience of time. Vonnegut summarizes Billy's life from his birth (1922) to the present (1968). Then he opens up two important plot lines. The first involves Billy's attempt to tell his story to the world in 1968. The second is the beginning of Billy's adventures in the war.

Vonnegut begins with the premise that Billy Pilgrim is "unstuck in time," that he lives his life out of sequence, paying random visits to all the events of his life, in no apparent order, and often more than once. But notice the two words "he says." Vonnegut uses them three times in this section, and they warn you that what Billy says may not always be fact.

Billy's "official biography" condenses Billy's life into the space of a couple of pages. It resembles the diagram Vonnegut drew for his Dresden story, which reduced Dresden to a few colored lines on the back of a length of wallpaper. And the biography serves the same purpose as the diagram: it allows you to see the whole story at a glance.

NOTE: Autobiography There are parallels here to Vonnegut's own life. He too was born in 1922, married and went to college after the war, and worked in Schenectady, an upstate New York city much like Ilium. We already know that he was captured by the Germans in World War II and lived through the bombing of Dresden. He is also over six feet tall.

The thumbnail sketch of Billy's life provides a framework into which you can fit the out-of-sequence events of the novel. Clearly *Slaughterhouse-Five* is not going to be just another "good story." For Vonnegut there is more than one aspect to any event: there is the event *itself*, how it is *experienced*, how it is *remembered* afterward, and, perhaps most important, how it is *told*.

NOTE: Multiple perspective   It can be maddening to have to be aware of all these levels at once. But Vonnegut's point is that you can't fully understand the story until you realize that all these levels exist *simultaneously* in any story. In effect you are being encouraged to look at *Slaughterhouse-Five* in the way a Tralfamadorian would—from every point of view, all at the same time.

Billy's biography ends in 1968, the "present," and Billy is writing to his local newspaper about the aliens who kidnapped him the year before.

Are the Tralfamadorians "real"? Vonnegut speaks of them as though Billy's account is to be taken seriously. But he's already cast doubt on Billy's credibility with those repeated "he says." Notice, too, that Billy never mentions the Tralfamadorians until after the plane crash. This makes it possible, even likely, that he imagined them in his delirium. The trauma to his brain, as often happens, has released vivid memories as well as hallucinations. This could mean that Billy's "coming unstuck in time" didn't happen in 1944, as it seems to him, but in 1968, when his skull was cracked. Certainly this is his daughter's interpretation of her father's stories. And not only has he gone soft in the head, he's determined to disgrace both himself and her by proclaiming his lunacy to the world!

In the middle of their argument Vonnegut stops the action to provide exposition—background information to help you understand what's going on—and to remind his readers that this is a story, not real life. Every chapter is studded with similar moments in which Vonnegut holds up the development of the story to indicate what he's doing as a writer.

NOTE: Exposition In a conventional story the author tries to weave the exposition into the action. Usually this is done by making what happens in the scene so engrossing that you're not aware you're being given bits of necessary information. But Vonnegut believes that a writer can't separate his telling of the story from the story itself. In Chapter 1 he went to a lot of trouble to demonstrate this problem. And one way to deal with the problem is to acknowledge it. Vonnegut is saying, We need exposition here, so here's the exposition.

The second plot line opens in the Luxembourg forest, where Billy and his companions—two infantry scouts and the antitank gunner Roland Weary—are lost behind enemy lines. It is here that Billy will first "come unstuck in time."

It's hard to imagine anyone more different from Billy Pilgrim than Roland Weary. In different circumstances these two might remind you of an incongruous comedy team. To the scouts, who are "clever, graceful, quiet" (perfectly adapted to their predicament), they aren't funny, they're dangerous: Weary because he makes so much noise, Billy because he just stands there when somebody shoots at him. If this were an ordinary war story, the scouts—who are expert soldiers—would probably be the main characters, Billy and Weary the comic relief. But Vonnegut is more interested in the clowns than in the good soldiers, perhaps because to him the clowns behave more like real people would. He is also preparing us for the irony in the next chapter, when the good soldiers will be killed and the clowns spared.

NOTE: Allusions and Parodies   In this scene Vonnegut makes some complex literary allusions or indirect references to other works. The name "Billy" recalls the innocent victim/hero of Herman Melville's *Billy Budd*. "Pilgrim" suggests John Bunyan's seventeenth-century moralistic novel, *Pilgrim's Progress*, in which the hero, called Christian, encounters many adventures and setbacks on his journey from the world of sin to the foot of the cross, where he finds salvation. All of Billy's story might be seen as a parody (take-off) of *Pilgrim's*

Progress: Billy passes through absurd scenes of modern life to find happiness among aliens from outer space.

The scene in the Luxembourg forest also parodies the conclusion of the medieval French epic poem *The Song of Roland*. (Vonnegut even tips you off to the allusion in Roland Weary's name.) In that war tale the protagonist and his best friend die heroically defending Western (i.e. Christian) civilization against attack by Muslim Saracens. The parody is quite detailed. The medieval Roland has a horn that he refuses to blow until he's really in trouble, while Weary has a whistle he won't blow until he is promoted to corporal. Roland is a true Christian fighting the infidel (non-believing) Saracen. Weary, a smelly footsoldier who doesn't know what he's fighting for, is up against the Nazis, the modern-day infidels.

Vonnegut makes it clear that Roland Weary can't help being an obnoxious jerk any more than Billy Pilgrim can help looking like a filthy flamingo. Weary's life has been a disaster because people are always "ditching" him, so he compensates by fantasizing an adventure in which he is a hero. Some readers see in this a parallel to Billy's fantasy of the Tralfamadorians, who choose him to represent the human race in their zoo. But it's also just common psychology. How many times have you felt "left out" and dreamed of doing something extraordinary that would "show" the people who snubbed you?

Notice the difference between Weary's "Three

Musketeers ˙ movie" which is full of violence, triumph, and manly camaraderie, and Billy's gentle, noncompetitive fantasies. Billy wins friends by sock skating and influences people by taking a public-speaking course.

Left to himself, Billy would have frozen to death days ago. So it may be stress that brings on his first slip in time. Many people who have come back from the brink of death have described the experience of having their whole life flash before their eyes. This comes pretty close to Vonnegut's description of Billy's "coming unstuck." Billy passes into death, moves backward to pre-birth, reverses direction again, and stops at the memory of a traumatic experience in his childhood. Then too he almost died because he wouldn't do anything to save himself.

Billy's next three stops in time are definitely in the future—Vonnegut even gives the dates. You're now inside Billy's experience of time, and it's perfectly real to him. You'll need to treat it as real from now on, or you'll miss a lot.

Billy is snapped back to the "present" by Roland Weary, for whom the dreaded moment has come. The scouts have abandoned him. Billy Pilgrim must now fulfill the destiny Weary has been keeping him alive for, that of sacrificial victim to Weary's "tragic wrath." The speech Weary makes while he's beating Billy up echoes speeches in *The Song of Roland* and other heroic epics. (Notice also the machine imagery Vonnegut uses to describe Billy's body: his spine is a *tube* containing all of Billy's important *wires*.

Before Weary can kill Billy for ruining his "movie," the Germans appear.

CHAPTER 3

Structure: Billy Pilgrim's time-travel now begins in earnest. In this chapter Billy jumps back and forth between 1944 and 1967. Each time he travels from one time period to the other, he picks up the new scene where he left off. While we alternate between two stories, then, the story in each period is continuous. Later on Billy's trips to the future will be much less orderly, but the continuity of the Dresden story will remain unbroken, for it is the dominant event of his life. In terms of the structure of the book, everything is anchored (as Billy is) to the Dresden story. You will always return to it, no matter how far away events may take you.

NOTE: To keep track of Billy's travels, you may want to do what Vonnegut did with his crayons and wallpaper: draw a diagram. To do this for each chapter, just skim through it to find out where Billy goes, then plot his time jumps on a graph.

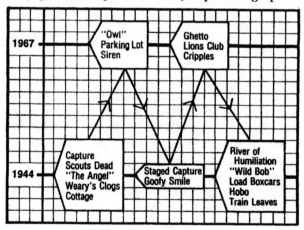

1967 — "Owl" Parking Lot Siren — Ghetto Lions Club Cripples

1944 — Capture Scouts Dead "The Angel" Weary's Clogs Cottage — Staged Capture Goofy Smile — River of Humiliation "Wild Bob" Load Boxcars Hobo Train Leaves

At each location, put in a key word or two to remind you of what happens in that scene. This will
not only give you the big picture of each chapter,
it may help you to find connections between images or events you hadn't seen before.

You may have noticed in Chapter 2 that each
scene Billy visits is related in some way to the one
he has just left. He's near death in the forest, then
he jumps to another scene in which he nearly dies.
His father is in one scene, his mother is in the
following one. This process resembles stream-of-
consciousness thinking: one idea somehow leads
to another. Everyone has experienced this process,
if only while daydreaming.

When you're worried or upset, certain images
or scenes keep returning to your mind, either to
replay themselves over and over or to pick up where
you left off. When you're only daydreaming, two
thoughts or scenes may be related by analogy
(something in one scene is the same as or like
something in the next) or by contradiction (something in one scene is the opposite of something in
the next).

In the worried variety of stream-of-conscious-
ness thinking, some images exert more pressure
than others. They keep recurring even when you've
drifted far away. Some of Billy's time jumps have
a whimsical quality that indicates that they are of
the carefree variety. But many times Billy returns
to a moment in his life as if to finish out the scene.
In such cases you can be pretty sure that it's psychological pressure that sends Billy there.

The Germans who capture Billy and Roland
Weary in the creek bed aren't at all what you'd

expect. They're a ragtag handful of ill-clad teen-
agers and old men with no teeth. Even their dog
seems incompetent. But they have the guns, and
they strip Weary down until he looks as embarrassing as they do. In the distance other German
soldiers take care of the American scouts with "three
inoffensive bangs."

Billy seems to find the whole scene comforting,
even beautiful, but then he's almost freezing to
death and hallucinating wildly. After being marched
to a stone cottage where he immediately falls asleep,
Billy pays a brief call on the future. It's almost as
though he's on reconnaissance, looking for a nice
time in his life to visit. The year 1967 is peaceful
enough in Ilium: it's business as usual in his office
in the shopping center. The only excitement comes
when the siren goes off. Billy thinks it's World War
III, but it's only noon.

NOTE: The imagery in almost every scene in this
chapter is ironic. Every time he wakes up in peaceful Ilium in 1967, he's reminded of war (the siren,
the devastated ghetto, the speech about Vietnam
by the Marine major, the crippled veterans), yet
each time he returns to World War II in 1944,
everything looks beautiful, and the togetherness
of the POWs is genuinely comforting to him. Vonnegut may be hinting that war has its good aspects, just as peace has its disadvantages.

He returns to 1944 and lets some German soldiers take pictures of him. This is kind of fun, but
something about 1967 has snagged him, and he

drifts back. Perhaps it's a premonition of the destruction he's about to see in the war, for Billy wakes up in his car in the middle of the Ilium ghetto, surrounded by burned-out buildings and crushed sidewalks. The area looks "like Dresden after it was firebombed—like the surface of the moon."

Billy is on his way to a luncheon at a popular American men's club that has for its symbol the most ferocious beast of the jungle, the lion. There he hears a Marine major talk of "bombing North Vietnam back into the Stone Age, if it refused to see reason." Billy isn't bothered because he has a prayer that keeps him from getting too upset about things:

> God grant me the serenity to accept the things
> I cannot change, courage to change the things
> I can, and wisdom always to tell the difference.

This "Prayer for Discernment" was composed by Reinhold Niebuhr (1892–1971), a German-American theologian. It is also the motto of Alcoholics Anonymous, whose members say they find it as comforting and useful as Billy's patients do.

NOTE: Vonnegut may be using the prayer here because it reinforces our impression of Billy Pilgrim as a passive character. He may also be making a veiled reference to his own alcoholism, which he hints at in Chapter 1. (Vonnegut no longer drinks, by the way.) The prayer will turn up again near the end of the book.

We learn now that Billy has a troubling problem

that belies his outward serenity: he has fits of weeping that he can't explain. Something is bothering Billy Pilgrim that all the riches and respect in his life cannot cure. If you suspect that it has something to do with his war experience, you're probably right.

As if to confirm this suspicion, Billy returns to the war. And now you understand another aspect of Billy's time-travel: when he can't bear to look at something that is happening at one time in his life, he dodges into another. In 1967 Billy is confronted by the disturbing spectacle of two crippled veterans selling phony magazine subscriptions. But back in 1944 he sees the world in a beautiful new way: everything is haloed by Saint Elmo's fire.

NOTE: Saint Elmo is the patron saint of sailors, who sometimes see a flamelike radiance surrounding the prominent points of a ship in stormy weather. Another name for this phenomenon is *corposant*, which comes from the Latin *corpus sancti*, meaning "body of a saint." Billy is having a kind of religious experience in which everything appears to be glowing with holiness.

The sights fill him with joy and excitement even though nobody else seems to be taking it this way—certainly not Roland Weary, whose feet are literally killing him.

The Americans' humiliation at being captured is made worse by the discomfort and boredom of being packed into boxcars with nothing to do for days. When you see prisoners in war movies, they are

usually either being tortured or planning escape.
(That is Roland Weary's kind of thinking.) Yet the
reality of being a prisoner of war is far less glam-
orous, and the details in this scene are as mundane
as they can be.

There are, however, the comforts of human con-
tact. The men sleep together "nestled like spoons."
They keep their courage up by yelling at the guards
(which is perfectly safe because the guards don't
understand English) and by telling each other it's
not so bad. One former hobo says he's seen lots
worse than this.

But it's dehumanizing to be a prisoner, however
peaceful and even domestic this scene may seem.
Vonnegut emphasizes this by injecting images that
depersonalize the prisoners. Trains talk to each other
across the rail yard, and "each car became a single
organism which ate and drank and excreted through
its ventilators."

After a while Vonnegut doesn't even refer to the
characters as prisoners or Americans; he simply
calls them human beings. Then he depersonalizes
them further: they are no longer individuals but
"a warm, squirming, farting, sighing earth" on the
floor of the boxcar.

Christmas passes unnoticed as the train moves
slowly east across Germany. And Billy Pilgrim
comes unstuck again.

CHAPTER 4

Structure: In this chapter we visit two time locations: 1967, when Billy is kidnapped by aliens,
and 1945, where we find out more of what it's like

to be a prisoner. Two important characters, Edgar Derby and Paul Lazzaro, make their appearance.

NOTE: Science Fiction   Early in the eighteenth century the French philosopher Montesquieu wanted to criticize his society and government. He thought that people would pay more attention to what he wrote if he invented visitors from a distant country who wrote "letters" home describing what they found in France. *The Persian Letters* was a best seller, and everyone talked about what the "Persians" had said about the French.

By the end of the nineteenth century, writers had found that other human beings, no matter what country they came from, did not provide enough contrast for the studies of human society they had in mind. So they invented creatures from other worlds, who would see the common, everyday behavior of human beings in an entirely different way. Thus, one purpose of science fiction is to encourage you to examine aspects of human activity that you normally take for granted and rarely think about.

The scene that opens Billy's first Tralfamadore story is littered with images that echo earlier scenes. The orange and black stripes on the wedding tent repeat the markings on the POW train. Billy and Valencia are "nestled like spoons in their big double bed," just as the prisoners were in the boxcar. Billy's blue and ivory feet recall the feet of corpses he saw on his way to the train. And the atmosphere of the sleeping house is reminiscent of Vonnegut's late-night vigil in Chapter 1.

There are more parallels, and all of them enhance the spookiness of the scene. Billy knows that in an hour something incredible is going to happen. To pass the time, and perhaps calm his nerves a little, he drinks flat champagne and watches a movie.

The World War II movie seen backward is one of the most famous passages in *Slaughterhouse-Five*. The idea is so simple—like a child's asking, "Daddy, why do people hurt each other?"—that it's amazing no one thought of it before. Have you ever done something in anger and later wished you could take it back? If life were a movie, Vonnegut is saying, that would be easy. You'd just run the film backward.

Billy doesn't stop going backward when he reaches the beginning of the movie and the soldiers have become high school kids. He wants to go all the way back to the beginning of human life and start over because he feels that human beings have messed things up the first time around.

Billy continues to be haunted by images from earlier experiences. A dog barks, just as one did in the Luxembourg forest before he was captured by the Germans. The ladder let down from the flying saucer looks like the rim of a Ferris wheel from his childhood. And the purple light he is trapped in is like the violet light of death.

Billy gets his first lesson in Tralfamadorian philosophy. When he asks, "Why me?" they answer:

"That is a very *Earthling* question to ask, Mr. Pilgrim. Why *you*? Why *us* for that matter? Why *anything*? Because this moment simply *is*. Have you ever seen bugs trapped in amber? . . .

"Well, here we are, Mr. Pilgrim, trapped in the amber of this moment. There is no *why*."

The bugs-in-amber comparison reminds us of characters trapped in diagrams in Chapter 1, and we can see that Vonnegut is drawing a parallel between human beings in time and characters in a story. To the Tralfamadorians, all time is fixed like a solid block of amber. Likewise a story is fixed once it is in print.

The saucer's takeoff dislodges Billy in time, and he goes back to the boxcar, which is slowly crossing Germany. As with Vonnegut during the nonnight he spent in Boston, time won't pass for Billy Pilgrim. One of the hardest things prisoners have to bear are the long stretches of empty time. Billy can measure time only by the click the wheels make as they go over a seam in the track. And a year passes between clicks, a direct echo of Chapter 1.

NOTE: Imprisonment and Deprivation A person placed in an environment of sensory deprivation quickly loses all sense of time, and this loss may be followed by more serious psychological disturbances such as hallucination, distortion of body image (parts of your body seem to blow up to giant size or shrink away to nothing, you can't find your arm, etc.), and vertigo (the ground seems to pitch and roll beneath you). This is why solitary confinement in a dark cell is considered such cruel punishment.

If Billy could sleep, he could do something interesting, like dream or travel in time. No one wants to sleep near him because he kicks and makes noise. Meanwhile, things are getting worse: there's no more food and the temperature is dropping. The optimistic former hobo dies, insisting "this ain't so bad." Roland Weary also dies, still blaming Billy for their capture and now for his death as well.

Vonnegut continues to employ dehumanizing images. The mass of prisoners are a liquid that the guards must coax into flowing out of the boxcars when they reach the prison camp.

Edgar Derby and Paul Lazzaro now appear, and Vonnegut introduces them impersonally as the best and worst *bodies*. Yet he gives each one a history so that you'll have to pay attention to these individual molecules of liquid flowing through the delousing station.

Derby not only has the best body, he seems to have the best reason for being here: he wanted to fight in this war. He is an educated, intelligent, and compassionate person (he cradled the dying Roland Weary). And we know already that Derby will die in Dresden.

NOTE: Edgar Derby is important to *Slaughterhouse-Five* in several ways. Vonnegut gives his age as forty-four (or forty-five) at the time of his capture in 1944, which means that he was born at the close of the nineteenth century. And Derby has the ideals and gentlemanly behavior that we usually associate with an older, more graceful era. We imagine that this elegant and honorable way of life died a horrible death as a result of two monstrous wars. Could it be a coincidence that Billy Pilgrim is himself forty-four in 1967, when he imagines he is kidnapped by aliens? At that age, many men go through an emotional trauma known as "the mid-life crisis," when they have to come to terms with the fact that they're no longer young. Edgar Derby may be fighting to prove that he *is* still young by keeping in shape and finagling his way into combat. Billy Pilgrim resolves his mid-life crisis by inventing aliens and time-travel.

And then perhaps the author just thinks that forty-four is an important age to be. Kurt Vonnegut was forty-four when he revisited Dresden in 1967.

Paul Lazzaro will turn out to have a personality as disgusting as his body. For the moment all we know is that he promised Weary he would get even with Billy Pilgrim.

Billy comes unstuck in time again in the stinging, impersonal shower. He wakes up in the flying saucer, having returned to where the first part of the chapter left off. Here he has his second lesson in the Tralfamadorian view of time and the universe: the question of free will does not exist beyond the civilization of Earth.

NOTE: Free Will   The doctrine of free will holds that the choices a human being makes are his own and they have a part in shaping his future. (The opposite of free will is determinism, which says that an individual's choices have already been made for him and he is powerless to change his future.) Philosophers (both theologians and lay people) have debated the existence of free will ever since the beginning of philosophy. But what was a burning question throughout most of human history seems to have little relevance for most people in the second half of the twentieth century. Do you know anyone who is concerned about whether or not free will exists?

The Tralfamadorian view does not accept or deny free will. It simply isn't an issue for them. Their concept of time and the universe is altogether different. Vonnegut may be saying here that the question of free will no longer has meaning.

CHAPTER 5

Structure: Chapter 5 is the longest in the book. It contains no less than thirteen time jumps. Billy's story develops significantly on three fronts: he arrives at the zoo on Tralfamadore, where he learns about the aliens' philosophy; as a POW in 1945 he reaches the prison camp and spends a crazy night on morphine, which gives him strange visions; and in a new time period, 1948, he appears in a mental hospital in Lake Placid, New York, where's he's recovering from a nervous breakdown, and later in a honeymoon resort with his new bride. As you read through the chapter, notice how Vonnegut enriches these plot developments by using echoes and analogies. He also introduces new material: an elaborate discussion of the effect fiction has on our understanding of life, a couple of drawings, and Billy's fantasy lover Montana Wildhack.

First, look at a couple of images that echo material from previous chapters. Under morphine in the prison camp, Billy has another of his peaceful hallucinations. It is similar to those he had in the Luxembourg forest just before his capture. This time he's a giraffe in a beautiful garden, and the only violence in the scene is Billy's chewing on a tough pear. Some readers see the giraffe as the perfect image for Billy Pilgrim: tall, gangling, absurdly gentle. For others, the giraffes represent a metaphor for human beings, creatures who are as "preposterously specialized" as giraffes. Remember how bizarre the Tralfamadorians find Earthlings, with their weird view of time and their curious ideas like free will? For Billy the heart of this vision seems to be his finding others like himself and being loved and accepted just as he is.

Another scene full of echoes is Billy's wedding night. After making love, Valencia wants to talk about the war. "It was a simple-minded thing for a female Earthling to do, to associate sex and glamor with war." Vonnegut's comment reminds us of Roland Weary's "sexy, murderous relationship" with his victims and of the German soldiers' mopping up "after the orgasm of victory."

Vonnegut spends most of this chapter examining fiction from many angles. The description he gives of Tralfamadorian literature (see the discussion of Style) sounds pretty familiar to someone who is reading *Slaughterhouse-Five*. Vonnegut had already announced on the title page that "this is a novel somewhat in the telegraphic schizophrenic manner of tales of the planet Tralfamadore, where the flying saucers come from," and now he explains what he meant. He also seems to be telling you what you should get from the book and how you can best appreciate and understand it.

On the other hand, you're not a Tralfamadorian. You can't read the brief clumps of symbols "all at once, not one after the other," so you can't appreciate "the depths of many marvelous moments seen all at one time." What kind of game is Vonnegut playing? It could be that he's harping on the difficulty of his Dresden story again: even if he could *write* it right, you couldn't *read* it right.

But there's another way of interpreting this. You can't read *Slaughterhouse-Five* the way a Tralfamadorian would, but when you think about the novel *after* you've read it, you can come close to seeing the book from a Tralfamadorian perspective. The entire story is then in your memory. You can focus on a favorite scene or image and move on to another part of the book without having to flip pages or read through the passages in between. You can go backward as well as forward in your memory of the story. And this applies not only to *Slaughterhouse-Five* but to any other work of fiction—and ultimately to all your past experiences as well.

Back in the prison camp the English officers give a performance of *Cinderella*, which Vonnegut calls "the most popular story ever told."

NOTE: Cinderella In *Palm Sunday*, Vonnegut says he believes that one of the reasons the Cinderella story is so popular has to do with its design. The structure of its plot is the same as that of the basic story of Christianity. The Old Testament creation myth parallels the gifts from Cinderella's fairy godmother, the expulsion from the Garden of Eden is the clock striking twelve, and the prince finding Cinderella is the redemption of the world by Jesus Christ. Both stories are so comforting and hopeful that they're hard to resist. Vonnegut maintains that any story with this structure is bound to be pop-

ular because people want so much to believe that
life works this way.

Many readers find Vonnegut's clearest statements on fiction in the scenes in the mental ward
in 1948. Here Billy discovers a kindred spirit in
Eliot Rosewater. Billy and Eliot are "alarmed by
the outside world." They have found life meaningless, in part because of their experiences in the
war. Both are "trying to re-invent themselves and
their universe" by reading science fiction.

NOTE: In his book *The Birth of Tragedy* the German philosopher Friedrich Nietzsche (1844–1900)
puts forth the idea that "only through art is life
justified." To him, life in itself is amoral and sense-
less. But art, he says, gives life meaning and purpose by *structuring* it—for example, by putting it
in the form of a story (myth, legend, fiction) that
has a beginning, a middle, and an end. Vonnegut
seems to like this idea, although he's not sure
whether it works any more.

According to Rosewater, Fyodor Dostoevsky's
The Brothers Karamazov contains everything there is
to know about life. One of the themes of that Russian masterwork is that the world is indeed terrifying because it has rejected God and tried to set
up man in God's place. But the implied solution
of that book—a return to faith—is what Rosewater
thinks "isn't *enough* any more."

He finds some consolation in science fiction,

particularly in the stories of Kilgore Trout, and he shares this discovery with Billy. Vonnegut summarizes two Kilgore Trout novels. In *Maniacs in the Fourth Dimension*, Trout proposes that certain mental illnesses have their causes in the "fourth dimension." Doctors can't really help because being Earthlings, they can see only in three dimensions.

NOTE: The Fourth Dimension Both Trout and Vonnegut use the term "fourth dimension" to indicate a vague aspect of the universe that is beyond human perception (which is limited to three dimensions, length, width, and depth). But modern physics, in particular Albert Einstein's theory of relativity, routinely uses a fourth dimension in its equations and calculations. This fourth dimension is called time. Trout's diagnosis seems to be correct in the case of Billy Pilgrim, who has so much trouble with time.

In *The Gospel from Outer Space* an alien visitor to Earth believes that Christians sometimes behave cruelly (as in the Crusades) because of "slipshod storytelling in the New Testament." So he writes a new Gospel in which Jesus isn't the Son of God until just before his death, when God adopts him. By changing this simple story element, the visitor from outer space "re-invents" Christianity.

These two fictitious novels of Kilgore Trout are clearly intended as satire: *Maniacs* sends up the "science" of psychology, *The Gospel* parodies the Scriptures. At the same time, both "fictions" explain mysteries that official theory or storytelling cannot account for. Vonnegut's point seems to be that fiction can be powerful in shaping the way you look at life and in helping you to understand things that otherwise would not make sense. Try to think of other books you've read that have changed the way you look at the world.

Vonnegut also examines two devices that fiction writers use: euphemism and metaphor. Notice Vonnegut's language in the story of Edgar Derby's capture. Shrapnel is turned into ordinary domestic objects, "knives and needles and razorblades," that rain down from "the incredible artificial weather Earthlings sometimes create for other Earthlings when they don't want those other Earthlings to inhabit Earth any more." There are no bullets per se, just "little lumps of lead in copper jackets . . . zipping along much faster than sound." These images are examples of *euphemism*, the "nice" way of describing something unpleasant. You may recall the "three inoffensive bangs" when the scouts were killed. The discrepancy between the terrifying reality and the innocent description of it relays the message more effectively than a straightforward description.

Each of these images is also a *metaphor*, a figure of speech in which a writer uses a word or a phrase to suggest a likeness or an analogy. A hilarious example of the necessity and absurdity of metaphors can be found in the scene in the alien zoo. The Tralfamadorians wonder what it must look like to be able to see in only three dimensions. The zoo guide explains Billy's plight by inventing the metaphor of a horribly complicated contraption that restricts Billy.

There are other new elements in this chapter

besides the discussion of fiction. On Billy's wedding night, while Valencia is trying to get him to talk about the war, he suddenly has an idea for his epitaph: "Everything was beautiful, and nothing hurt." What's odd about this is that Vonnegut provides a drawing to go with the words. Then, in the very next scene, there's another drawing, this time of the latrine sign that Billy—in his morphine haze—sees floating in midair: "Please leave this latrine as tidy as you found it!" Vonnegut's drawings of the two messages make them seem pretty important, for these are the first drawings to appear in the book. Perhaps the second drawing is meant as a contrast to the first, which expresses Billy's hopelessly naive idea of what life should be like—the latrine sign is meant to bring you down to earth, as it were. It's also possible that the second drawing is philosophical advice from the author: "Life is enough of a mess, don't make it worse."

Chapter 5 also introduces Montana Wildhack, Billy's mate in the zoo on Tralfamadore. As fantasy, Billy's love story with Montana is hard to beat from a male point of view. She is vulnerable, trusting, and above all beautiful. Billy can be her gallant protector. She takes the sexual initiative—shyly, of course—with the result that Billy doesn't need to feel any guilt about having "taken advantage of her." But even in this paradise Billy can't entirely forget the war. The shadow of her naked body on the wall reminds him of the skyline of Dresden before it was bombed.

A curious thing occurs near the end of the chapter. The scene in which Billy takes the train to Ilium for his father's funeral ends on the platform, with Billy talking to the porter. In the next paragraph Vonnegut returns to Billy's morphine night in the prison camp. The narrator says nothing about Billy's traveling in time. Before this the jumps Billy made in time were told in the order in which they occurred, but now Vonnegut interrupts the sequence of Billy's time-travels.

It's unlikely that Vonnegut forgot what he was doing. More probably the war story, as the novel approaches Dresden, is exerting more psychological pressure.

CHAPTER 6

Structure: With one important exception—Billy's vision of his own assassination in 1976—the war months are the scene of the entire chapter. And at last the American POWs arrive in Dresden, where the most significant event in Billy's life will take place.

The chapter begins with another break in the sequence of Billy's time-travels. Chapter 5 ended in 1968, Chapter 6 begins on the morning after Billy's morphine night in the prison camp. The short opening scene is a little hard to believe, even by Billy Pilgrim's standards. It could be that the lingering effects of the morphine make Billy think that the two lumps in the lining of his new coat are secret treasures that are radiating a message for him. It could also be Vonnegut's whimsical comment on the strange power that hidden treasure sometimes exerts over men.

Billy sleeps for a while, then is awakened by the racket the English officers are making in building a new latrine, the Americans having ruined the old one.

NOTE: The "Golgotha sounds" Billy hears are a reference to the hill in Jerusalem where Jesus was crucified. The name means "place of the skull." The six men carrying the pool table like pallbearers add to this morbid image.

Paul Lazzaro delivers a sermonette on "the sweetest thing there is": revenge. He tells Billy and Derby a gruesome story about how he got back at a dog that bit him (maybe that's where he got the rabies!), and he advises Billy to enjoy life while he can. You learn now of the spiritual kinship between Lazzaro and his one war buddy, the late Roland Weary. Lazzaro has promised the dying Weary to get the man who killed him, and everyone who was in Weary's boxcar knows that it was Billy Pilgrim.

The next section, describing Billy's death, is peppered with the phrase "he says," an indication that this is one of Billy's fantasies. Notice that Billy doesn't travel there. Vonnegut simply holds up the war story to tell us what Billy Pilgrim says his death will be like.

NOTE: Vonnegut's Anti-Americanism Vonnegut's mockery of American values and behavior is pretty blatant throughout the whole prison camp sequence. First there was Billy's "vision of hell"— the Americans being "sick as volcanoes" after the feast and destroying the latrine. Then there was Campbell's so-called study of American POWs, which describes them as "the most self-pitying, least fraternal, and dirtiest of all prisoners of war." And in Billy's fantasy of the future, "The United States of America has been Balkanized, has been divided into twenty petty nations so that it will never again be a threat to world peace." This has led many of Vonnegut's critics to label him anti-American. His supporters argue that Vonnegut mocks America not because he hates it, but because he loves it so much, and wants his countrymen to be better than they are. What do you think?

Returning to the war, Billy is leaving the prison hospital with Lazzaro and Derby. Just as the three prisoners in their outlandish garb form "an unconscious travesty of that famous patriotic oil painting 'The Spirit of '76,' " what follows is a travesty of a free election. Edgar Derby becomes "head American." He gives an absurd acceptance speech, promising "to make damn well sure" everyone gets home safely. You can't miss the irony here or in the pathetic letters to his wife he's been composing in his head. Like Billy Pilgrim, you know already that Edgar Derby won't have anything to do with the safe return of his fellow prisoners. He'll be dead.

The scene has its bright moments. The prisoners learn they're being sent to Dresden, an "open city" that no one expects to be bombed. (In World War II, cities were declared "open" if they were considered to have no military value.) And Billy adds some touches of color to his frumpy outfit: an azure (light blue) toga and silver boots. He may once have looked like a filthy flamingo, but now he's a full-fledged clown.

Once they get to Dresden, Billy becomes the real leader of the Americans for all of Edgar Derby's "patriotism and middle age and imaginary wisdom." When the nervous guards finally see what the "murderous American infantrymen" are really like ("Here were more crippled human beings, more fools like themselves. Here was light opera"), they naturally put Billy at the head of the parade. He's the one best dressed for the part.

Not everybody thinks the Americans are funny. An exhausted surgeon demands to know how Billy has the nerve to look as clownish as he does. Billy makes the only friendly gesture he can think of in his dazed state of mind: he offers to the stranger his "treasures," the diamond and part of a denture that are hidden in his coat lining.

NOTE: Appearance   From a "civilized" standpoint, the surgeon is right to be offended. His outrage at how the Americans are dressed is the same as the outrage of the English officers. To these cultured Europeans, appearance is of the utmost importance: it is the flower of civilization. If the flower looks healthy, the whole plant must be sound. The English colonel at the prison camp was correct when he said "If you stop taking pride in your appearance, you will very soon die."

At last the narrative comes to the place that gives the book its name, and Billy arrives at the anchor point of his story. Here, beneath Slaughterhouse-Five (*Schlachthof-Fünf*), Billy will spend the night in which Dresden is destroyed.

It is almost with a sigh of relief that you reach Dresden after hearing about it for so long. Vonnegut has heightened the suspense by announcing the destination far in advance and then delaying (while he told the story) Billy's arrival in Dresden. The real "climax" of the story has yet to come, and you can be sure that Vonnegut will put that off for as long as he can.

CHAPTER 7

Structure: The story swings gently between two locations in time: the doomed airplane in 1968 and Dresden just before the bombing in 1945. When Chapter 7 opens, it's twenty-five years later than the close of Chapter 6. The narrator seems to have taken over the storytelling controls from Billy Pilgrim and is deciding on his own the order in which scenes will be presented. This short chapter also offers contrasting views of relations between people of different nationalities.

The plane's takeoff is unremarkable, except for the irony of Valencia's eating a candy bar as she waves goodbye to Billy for the last time. You know they will never see each other again—at least not in Earthling time.

Once in the air, the optometrists begin to party. Billy's father-in-law, Lionel Merble, gets things going by asking the barbershop quartet, The Febs (an anagram of Four-eyed Bastards), to sing his favorite naughty songs. The racist ditties that Lionel Merble finds so hilarious are followed by a scene in which a Polish man is hanged for having sex with a German woman during the war.

NOTE: Nazi Racism The law the Pole had broken was one of many "race laws" instituted by Adolf Hitler and his minister for propaganda, Joseph Goebbels. Hitler believed that Germans were the "master" race, the "Aryans," and he made any mixing with inferior races a capital crime. The most famous victims of the race laws were the Jews, but anyone not of pure "Aryan" ancestry was in danger of being persecuted by the Nazis. One of Vonnegut's aunts, in order to marry a *German* German in the 1930s, had to prove that she had no "mixed blood" in her family.

Billy's brief time-travel to the Luxembourg forest just before the plane crashes indicates a parallel between the two incidents: in both cases Billy is the only survivor. The "guys" do indeed "go on" without him! In 1968 Billy is rescued by Austrian ski instructors who look like "golliwogs" in their ski masks.

NOTE: A golliwog was a doll whose face caricatured the features of a black person. Golliwogs first appeared in Florence K. Upton's illustrations for a series of children's books in the late nineteenth century. Here the racist image ties in with Lionel Merble's vulgar songs and the execution of the Pole for interracial sex.

Billy thinks he's back in the war, which seems to have entered a new technological phase: there are colorful uniforms and huge machines that swing people through the sky.

When he returns to the real war, Billy, Edgar Derby, and the sixteen-year-old "baby" who is guarding them, Werner Gluck, are on their way to supper in the slaughterhouse. (Werner's last name, ironically, means "good luck, happiness, prosperity" in German.) Because of blackout regulations, the city is not as beautiful as it would be in peacetime, and the stockyard and animal pens have long been empty. Otherwise, everything is serene.

They make a wrong turn and stumble upon a group of women taking showers. The sight of naked women is "nothing new to Derby," but Billy and Werner Gluck can only gape while the women become even more enchanting by screaming and trying to cover themselves. This recalls Billy's first sight of Montana Wildhack in the zoo on Tralfamadore. But there are dark undertones here as well: the women are refugees from a bombed-out city who have come to Dresden because it is "safe." You'll discover later that they perish in a shallow shelter and that others like them are boiled alive in a watertower.

The "three fools" finally find the kitchen, where an impatient war widow has been keeping their meal hot for them. Her anxiety to get home, even though there's nothing there but memories, doesn't stop her from caring about the people in her charge.

The last scene in this brief chapter is one of the most touching in the book. Despite what the English colonel had predicted, food in Dresden is scarce and not very nourishing. So the prisoners working in the factory that makes enriched malt syrup for pregnant women have been secretly spooning the syrup to sustain their own lives as well. The image of every cell in Billy's body shaking him "with ravenous gratitude and applause" for the spoonful of syrup is then repeated with Edgar Derby, who bursts into tears. That such a tiny thing could do so much is an indication of just how impoverished Dresden was at the time.

The chapter is filled with examples of people's feeding one another, saving and sustaining each other's lives. You see not only racism but instances of "international cooperation."

CHAPTER 8

Structure: Chapter 8 begins just days before the bombs fall on Dresden, and it ends on the day after the bombing, when the prisoners emerge from their shelter beneath the slaughterhouse. Billy meets Kilgore Trout in 1964 and undergoes a devastating experience that causes him to remember the awful event that has dominated his life. Thus he begins to come to terms with it.

In the slaughterhouse two days before the bombing, Howard W. Campbell, Jr., the American Nazi propagandist, is recruiting members for his Free American Corps. It's doubtful that the American POWs look like hot prospects to him.

As Vonnegut describes the Americans' attempt to stay awake for Campbell's presentation, he reverts again to impersonal imagery, calling Campbell's audience "it" and describing "its" symptoms of malnutrition. But Edgar Derby won't stand for either Campbell's nonsense or Vonnegut's dehumanization, and he distinguishes himself by staging a fine scene.

During the bombing alert that follows Edgar Derby's shining moment, Billy nods off and returns to the present, 1968, where his daughter is scolding him. Now she's blaming Kilgore Trout for filling Billy's head with nonsense.

Four years earlier Billy discovers Trout by accident in a back alley of Ilium, where Trout subsidizes his novel writing by working in the circulation department of a newspaper. Trout is flabbergasted at meeting someone who's actually read his books—and liked them! Billy is equally delighted, for Trout's books have helped him so much through the years. They become friends, and Billy invites Trout to attend his and Valencia's eighteenth anniversary party.

NOTE: The chronology here is confused. If this is 1964, then Billy and Valencia were married in 1946. But in Chapter 5 they're only engaged, and that's in 1948. So one of the dates is incorrect, or else it's not their eighteenth anniversary. The discrepancy probably isn't important. Calendars only measure external time, and you know how unreliable that can be.

Trout is the hit of the evening, the only author in a roomful of optometrists. And he's having the time of his life, bragging and posing and showing off shamelessly. He spends most of the party trying to impress Maggie White, a naive "airhead" who believes anything anybody tells her. She resembles

the hyped-up ads she believes in so wholeheart-
edly—"a sensational invitation to make babies" who
in fact uses birth control.

The barbershop quartet launches the presentation ceremony for Billy's anniversary gift to Valencia. But The Febs' singing upsets Billy so much
that he has to leave the room. No one understands
what has happened to Billy, though Trout believes
it's something strange, like seeing through a time
window. In a way this is exactly what has happened.

The real explanation is even more chilling than
the spookiest science fiction. The singing quartet
looks just like the four German guards when they
and the American POWs first saw Dresden after it
was bombed.

It's significant that Billy figures this out without
resorting to time-travel. Most of Billy's trips in time
have allowed him to escape from unpleasantness,
but by consciously *remembering* Dresden, Billy begins to be able to deal with his experience.

NOTE: Music often has a mnemonic effect, that
is, it triggers vivid memories. In Billy's case this is
enhanced by the shapes (shapes, like sounds, can
be mnemonic) of the singers' mouths because they
remind him so much of the expressions the guards
"try on" one after another. The absurdity of the
link in Billy's mind between the four guards and
the barbershop quartet is what makes it so moving.

And with that the time has come to relive, with
Billy and Vonnegut, the bombing of Dresden.

If you were writing *Slaughterhouse-Five*, how would you handle this scene? It's the climax of the story, the scene that must be effective or the rest of the book is pointless. The natural choice would be to try to make this moment as exciting and frightening as possible. But what does Vonnegut do? After all that buildup and suspense, you see nothing. You hear only "sounds like giant footsteps above" and the guards whispering about "one big flame." The only shock you feel is "an occasional shower of calcimine."

Some readers are disappointed by Vonnegut's failure to describe the bombing of Dresden more graphically. They feel that this scene is a horrible anticlimax and that they have been cheated.

For other readers, Vonnegut's account is perfect because he tells only what he himself experienced firsthand, and he was in the meat locker the entire time. Other firsthand reports come from similarly remote vantage points, such as the movies taken from the bombers. Vonnegut saw one of these films later. All he could say was, "The city appeared to boil" Anything "closer" would have to be as imaginary as a description of what it's like on the surface of the sun.

Those who are disappointed in this "anticlimax" also accuse Vonnegut of copping out, of failing to face up to the true horror of the Dresden bombing. They attribute this failure either to a lack of nerve or to a lack of talent.

Others argue that Vonnegut has the imagination and skill to have painted a vivid picture of the annihilation of Dresden if he'd wanted to. They believe that Vonnegut's indirect account is all the more effective because the horror remains—as it was for the survivors—too big to grasp.

However you feel about Vonnegut's account of the bombing of Dresden, the central event of the story is now past. But as anyone who has been seriously injured can tell you, the aftermath is often the worst part.

Vonnegut allows Billy to back away from reliving Dresden and to become a storyteller himself. Earlier, in the honeymoon scene, Billy was embarrassed by Valencia's questions about the war and ducked into the bathroom the first chance he got. Now, with Montana Wildhack in the zoo on Tralfamadore, he seems to have no such problems. Montana doesn't specify what story she wants to hear, and Billy's choice seems rather grim: the appearance of Dresden on the day after the bombing. Billy isn't running away from his Dresden experience any more. It's the most important story in his life, and he's no longer afraid of it.

Vonnegut closes the chapter with an account of the prisoners' first day in the "new" Dresden. After the initial shock and grief, the guards' survival instinct takes over and they start moving everyone toward the outskirts. American planes appear for the "mopping up," machine-gunning anything that moves. They miss Billy and Vonnegut's group but kill some people in another cluster of survivors by the river. Vonnegut's deadpan remark that "the idea was to hasten the end of the war" prepares us for dealing with this subject in the next chapter.

CHAPTER 9

Structure: In Chapter 9 Vonnegut wraps up all of Billy Pilgrim's stories except that of the immediate aftermath of the Dresden bombing. And he starts and finishes two new stories that take place in 1968. The first is Billy's encounter with Professor Rumfoord in the Vermont hospital. The second is his attempt to tell his story to the world by going on a radio talk show in New York City. Vonnegut also addresses the most important question about the bombing of Dresden: why?

He begins by removing Valencia. Because Billy is still delirious from the plane crash he is busy dreaming and traveling in time, and doesn't learn about his wife's death until later. Billy's hospital roommate, Professor Bertram Copeland Rumfoord, is busy with a project of his own: an official history of the army air force in World War II.

Rumfoord embodies in every way the old-fashioned ideal of the American male. Athletic, potent, and fiercely energetic even in his seventies, Rumfoord has worn out four wives and is working on a fifth, his new bride Lily, who was born in the year Dresden was bombed. Poor Lily is just a symbol to Rumfoord, "one more public demonstration that he was a superman." She has been running errands, collecting material for Rumfoord's book, even though she's supposed to be on her honeymoon. The document she brings in now is President Harry S. Truman's announcement that the first atomic bomb has just been dropped on Hiroshima.

NOTE: The Atomic Bomb   Vonnegut breaks off the quote just when Truman is about to give what many thought was the best reason for using the bomb—to hasten the end of the war. The rest of the announcement runs as follows:

> It was to spare the Japanese people from ut-

ter destruction that the ultimatum of July 26
[1945, calling for unconditional surrender] was
issued [by the U.S., Britain and Russia] at Pots-
dam. Their leaders promptly rejected that ultimatum. If they do not now accept our terms
they may expect a rain of ruin from the air, the
like of which has never been seen on earth.
Behind this air attack will follow sea and land
forces in such numbers and power as they have
not yet seen and with the fighting skill of which
they are already well aware.

Truman's statement sounds rather boastful today, but it must be remembered that America had
been at war for almost four years, and everyone
thought and spoke accordingly. In addition, although Japan was clearly losing the war, it still
remained capable of fierce resistance, as the fighting in the Pacific had demonstrated. The only alternative to dropping the bomb was a massive invasion, and that could have prolonged the fighting
for years, with tremendous loss of life on both sides.

Vonnegut presents contrasting official views of
the Dresden bombing. The first, written by a re-
tired Air Force general, sounds a lot like Truman's
in its reasoning, but the tone is definitely more
belligerent. The second, written by an Englishman
of equal rank, is calmer in its language. It desig-
nates Dresden as the worst massacre in history.

For readers who share his antiwar sympathies,
this section of Chapter 9 provides Vonnegut's most
devastating indictment of the military manner of
thinking. By having the "warmongers" speak, he
cleverly lets them damn themselves. Other readers
find Vonnegut's wholesale condemnation of vio-

lence under any circumstances simplistic and immature and accuse him of stacking the deck against people who sincerely wanted to end the war. These readers argue that once the fighting was under way, there were only two choices: destroy the enemy or surrender.

Billy Pilgrim is little concerned with these arguments. Neither his children nor Valencia's death seem to have much effect on him. Everyone thinks the brain damage has made him a vegetable, but the truth is quite the opposite. Billy is working on a project that has given purpose to his life: he is "preparing letters and lectures about the flying saucers, the negligibility of death, and the true nature of time." He believes he can save the world.

What brings Billy out of his creative trance is his roommate, Professor Rumfoord, who talks of putting Billy out of his misery. Billy tries to speak to him, but it's not easy to penetrate what Vonnegut calls Rumfoord's "military manner" of perceiving Billy.

Between bouts of "trying to prove to a willfully deaf and blind enemy that he was interesting to hear and see," Billy travels in time to his last adventure in Dresden. It's a warm spring day two days after the end of the war in Europe. Billy is snoozing in the back of a wagon. He has nowhere to go, nothing to do, and he is at peace with the world for the first and almost the last time in his life.

His peace is shattered when two German obstetricians wake him and scold him because he and his thoughtless buddies have badly abused the horses pulling the wagon. Billy bursts into tears. Do you see the connection with the previous scene?

Rumfoord is no worse for refusing to listen to Billy than Billy is for being oblivious to the horses' suffering. Thoughtlessness is not restricted to the "military manner" of thinking; human beings seem to be thoughtless by nature.

Billy returns in time to the Vermont hospital to finish dealing with Rumfoord, who offers a new bit of conventional wisdom about the massacre at Dresden: "Pity the men who had to *do* it"—as if the agents were more to be pitied than the victims.

NOTE: Rumfoord is obviously a caricature (an exaggerated, one-sided portrait) of the all-American male, so this statement sounds absurd coming from him. Vonnegut's own feelings on the subject are more complex. In an interview he relates the following story: "When I went to the University of Chicago after the war the guy who interviewed me for admission had bombed Dresden. He got to that part of my life story and he said, 'Well, we hated to do it.' The comment sticks in my mind. . . . [It] was more humane [than saying 'We were ordered to do it']. I think he felt the bombing was necessary, and it may have been."

Billy is beyond such considerations. He has transcended even the humaneness of the horse pitiers. He has The Answer: "Everything is all right, and everybody has to do exactly what he does. I learned that on Tralfamadore."

This sounds a lot like determinism, which was discussed in Chapter 4. If you recall the autobiographical elements in Billy Pilgrim's character and

the way Vonnegut has previously used the Tralfamadorians to make direct thematic statements,
it's tempting to see Vonnegut's answer to Dresden
as: it had to be. But remember that the author has
a larger perspective than Billy, larger even than the
Tralfamadorians. And don't forget how Vonnegut
brought Billy to this comforting philosophy: a plane
crash scrambled Billy's brains, disturbing his sense
of time and making him unable to tell the difference between real life and fantasy. This hardly
qualifies Billy as a wise man whose message should
be taken seriously.

By thus undermining Billy's credibility, Vonnegut may be attempting to answer those who de-
fend the Dresden bombing: it *may* have been necessary, as he admits, but there is no way to be
sure, unless you're an alien who can see in four
dimensions, or a prematurely senile optometrist
who thinks he's "come unstuck in time."

In order to deal with his Dresden experience,
Billy has literally gone out of his mind. What of
the author himself? How is Vonnegut coming to
terms with his memories of the war? The answer
must wait until both Billy's story and the story of
Vonnegut's writing *Slaughterhouse-Five* are complete, which will happen in the next chapter. For
the moment, Billy Pilgrim has a final adventure to
go through.

After coming home from the hospital, he sneaks
off to New York to proclaim his solution to all of
life's problems. He's tremendously excited, not only
by his mission but because it's almost the first time
in his life that he has been entirely on his own. He
goes to Times Square, and in a pornography shop
he finds books by Kilgore Trout. The one he re-

members having read is *The Big Board*, whose story is very similar to Billy's interlude with Montana Wildhack on Tralfamadore. Billy had read this book in the mental hospital after the war.

Another Trout novel is new to him: a time-traveler goes back to Biblical days to meet the real Jesus and find out whether or not Jesus died on the cross. Clearly Trout is very much interested in the Jesus story (remember *The Gospel from Outer Space?*). But then so is Vonnegut. There are allusions to Jesus throughout *Slaughterhouse-Five*. The horse pitiers were "crooning" to the horses, and their "tones might have been those used by the friends of Jesus when they took His ruined body down from His cross." And Vonnegut thinks the Christmas carol "Away in the Manger" describes Billy Pilgrim as well as Jesus.

Some readers think Vonnegut is mocking Christianity by parodying the myths on which it is based. Although he once attended services in a Unitarian Church more or less regularly, Vonnegut has been an atheist all his life and in general believes that organized religion is as dangerous as any other form of organized authority. Other readers maintain that Vonnegut makes a distinction between the *stories* and ideals that form the basis of religious faith and the religious *institutions* whose actions he finds are often atrocious.

Whatever you see as the cause of Vonnegut's ambivalence toward religion, his attitude toward pornography is pretty clear: "It was a ridiculous store, all about love and babies." Of course the so-called sex peddled here has nothing to do with love or babies.

Before you leave this charming establishment,

notice the references to Montana Wildhack. The blue movie in the peepshow machine was made when she was a teenager. The article about her disappearance is in an *old* magazine. Here's more evidence that Billy's time-travel and the Tralfamadore fantasy began after the plane crash. He had known about Montana Wildhack's disappearance from reading this magazine when it first appeared, and in his delirium in the Vermont hospital he put it together with the premise of *The Big Board*. And remember, that the alien visitor in *The Gospel from Outer Space* was "shaped very much like a Tralfamadorian." The evidence is circumstantial, but it all fits.

Billy finally gets on a radio talk show. In this scene, Vonnegut concludes his discussion of fiction. He began it in Chapter 1 by considering the difficulty of writing fiction in the first place. In Chapter 5 he examined the not always positive effect fiction has on one's ability to understand and cope with life. Here he mocks the pronouncements of the "experts" on literature.

NOTE: The Virginian Vonnegut refers to is William Styron, whose novel *The Confessions of Nat Turner* had recently been published. That book portrayed sympathetically the trials and tribulations of a black slave in the Old South, as had *Uncle Tom's Cabin* by Harriet Beecher Stowe, a Northerner, over a hundred years before.

"The death of the novel" was a fashionable topic at the time *Slaughterhouse-Five* was written, and Vonnegut spares little of his wit in deflating the pretentious attitudes of much literary criticism of the day.

For all his mocking tone in this section, Vonnegut has elsewhere voiced considerable doubt about the worth of fiction and its ability to say anything intelligent about the modern world. Billy's personal answer to the absurdity of contemporary life—he reinvents his life through fantasy —so embarrasses the panel of experts that they throw him out of the studio. Are they themselves any less embarrassing in their pompous seriousness, in Vonnegut's view? No, he seems to say, but they have a point, however absurdly they express it. Even if the novel isn't dead, it's not very healthy.

Little disturbed having his message rejected, Billy returns to his room and goes to bed so that he can visit Montana Wildhack one last time. By now they have a baby and Billy's wonderful fantasy is complete. He tells her about seeing her pictures in the Times Square porn shop, but she dismisses her past life as being as meaningless as his Dresden story. They have started the human race over again; the slate of the past is clean.

NOTE: The Drawings Vonnegut's drawing of the prayer inscribed on a locket hanging between Montana's breasts completes the trio of drawings in *Slaughterhouse-Five*. They are not just pictures, for each contains a message. The pattern of these messages is similar to a common formula in philosophical argument. First a thesis or idea is put forth: Life is nice ("Everything was beautiful, and nothing hurt"). Then the antithesis or opposing idea is laid out against it: Life is a mess ("Please leave this latrine as tidy as you found it!"). Finally a synthesis is achieved by combining the two into a meaningful whole: Life is both good and bad (the prayer). The prayer itself demonstrates this kind of structure: God grant me the serenity to accept the things I cannot change (thesis), courage to change the things I can (antithesis), and wisdom always to know the difference (synthesis).

Just as the tombstone in the first drawing is a symbol of death, the breasts in this last drawing are a symbol of life. They may also imply that the serenity, courage and wisdom asked for in the prayer can only be found in a nurturing, loving relationship with another person. The symbolism in this drawing is particularly rich, and you can probably find other meanings in it as well.

CHAPTER 10

Structure: This brief closing chapter falls roughly into two equal parts, the first part describing Vonnegut's return to Dresden with O'Hare in 1967, the second part closing out Billy Pilgrim's story with his last days as a POW in 1945, which he spends digging for bodies in the rubble.

Vonnegut begins by musing about recent violent deaths. As a conclusion to his musings, he remarks casually that the Tralfamadorians are more interested in Darwin than in Jesus. This is because the version of Darwin's theory of natural selection, commonly known as "survival of the fittest," accords with their determinism. Jesus was a crusader who tried to change things, which to the Tralfamadorians is impossible.

Vonnegut turns from talk of death to the subject of pleasant memories. One of his favorites is going to Dresden with O'Hare, this time for fun. And, in Vonnegut's case, for profit—but the irony is chilling. In a new introduction for *Slaughterhouse-Five*, written in 1976, he says:

> The Dresden atrocity, tremendously expensive and meticulously planned, was so meaningless, finally, that only one person on the entire planet got any benefit from it. I am that person. I wrote this book, which earned a lot of money for me and made my reputation, such as it is.
>
> One way or another, I got two or three dollars for every person killed. Some business I'm in.

Flying over the rebuilt cities of Germany, Vonnegut can't help imagining what it would look like if he dropped bombs on them.

The final sequence of scenes in the aftermath of the Dresden bombing is grim. The imagery is overwhelmingly dehumanized: the moonscape, the membrane of timbers, the corpse mines. Civilization has been so thoroughly wiped out that not even domestic animals can be used to help clean up the mess. Only human beings are adaptable and clever enough to deal with it.

Eventually the corpse mines are closed down. The job is simply too huge, and the soldiers have other things to do. Dresden is abandoned and all the weapons are buried.

As spring stubbornly appears, the Americans walk out into sudden freedom. The birds say the only intelligent thing there is to say about a massacre, "Poo-tee-weet"—that is, nothing!

One question that is left unanswered at the end of the book is what happens to Billy Pilgrim? Will he really be assassinated by Paul Lazzaro in 1976? Or does he escape permanently to Tralfamadore, to spend the rest of his days with his new family in a new Garden of Eden? (Notice that Vonnegut doesn't bring Billy back to Earth after his last scene with Montana.) Or are these just the fantasies of a deranged mind, and what really happens is that Barbara has her father locked up in an asylum? This seems the most likely answer to her question, "Father, Father, Father—What are we going to do with you?" You can find support for every one of these answers in different places in the novel, and Vonnegut never says which one he prefers.

This ambiguity is probably intentional. If Vonnegut could decide what to do with Billy Pilgrim, maybe he could tie up his own war experience into a neat little story as well, and he obviously can't—or won't—do that. Remember what he said in Chapter 1:

> [This book] is so short and jumbled and jangled, Sam, because there is nothing intelligent to say about a massacre. Everybody is supposed to be dead, to never say anything or want anything ever again. Everything is supposed to be very quiet after a massacre, and it always is, except for the birds.

Some readers believe that writing *Slaughterhouse-Five* was a form of therapy for Vonnegut. By the very act of putting his war experience into the structure of a story (no matter how unorthodox that structure may be), Vonnegut gives meaning to that otherwise absurd experience. This is similar to the idea that only through art is life justified. According to this view, Vonnegut is doing the same sort of thing in writing *Slaughterhouse-Five* that he has Billy Pilgrim do to cope with his war experience: Billy re-invents his life through fantasy and time-travel, Vonnegut by writing a novel.

Other readers find this interpretation too simplistic. True, they say, Vonnegut does re-invent his life in a way, by assuming the character of Billy Pilgrim, and then having Billy find a solution to all of his problems. But what kind of a solution is this—a retreat from reality into premature senility, and that is only possible after he's cracked his skull in a plane crash? Is Vonnegut really recommending such a course of action? To these readers, Vonnegut's "answer" to the meaningless horror of his war experience is just as meaningless as the experience itself.

Vonnegut may be saying that there is no way to completely lay an experience like Dresden to rest. And maybe he feels that it would be wrong to forget that horror, or to "re-invent" the memory of it so that it becomes just another "tale of great destruction." By combining the innocence of the "baby" who experienced it and the embarrassed perspective of the "old fart" who is trying to make sense of it, Vonnegut is keeping the memory of the Dresden massacre alive, perhaps in the hope that this may help to keep it from happening again.

A STEP BEYOND

Tests and Answers

TESTS

Test 1

1. Vonnegut had trouble writing *Slaughter-house-Five* because he ____
   A. couldn't remember any good stories about the war
   B. was distracted by other projects
   C. couldn't make sense of his Dresden experience

2. Billy's daughter Barbara is upset with him because ____
   A. she thinks he's crazy
   B. she doesn't want to take care of him
   C. his stories about aliens and time-travel embarrass her

3. The "river of humiliation" refers to ____
   A. the place where American planes machine-gunned survivors of the Dresden bombing
   B. the movement of POWs
   C. the passage of time

4. Roland Weary dies from ____
   A. gangrene in his feet
   B. starvation   C. exposure

5. Edgar Derby is much older than his fellow ____
   soldiers because he

A. used to be an officer
B. was drafted by mistake
C. pulled strings to get into the fighting

6. Eliot Rosewater is in the mental hospital _____
because
   A. he's an alcoholic
   B. he is alarmed by life
   C. he has no place else to go

7. Billy can't talk to his wife about the war _____
because
   A. he hates her   B. he is embarrassed
   C. she thinks he was a hero

8. Paul Lazzaro is going to have Billy killed _____
after the war because
   A. it was Billy's fault that Lazzaro was
      captured
   B. Billy broke Lazzaro's arm
   C. Roland Weary made Lazzaro promise it

9. The Dresden surgeon who scolds Billy is _____
angry because
   A. the Americans laugh at him
   B. he thinks Billy is treating the war as a
      joke
   C. he is exhausted

10. Valencia kills herself _____
    A. by accident
    B. because Billy doesn't love her
    C. because her life is meaningless

11. What is the significance of Tralfamadore in
    Slaughterhouse-Five?

12. Why is Kilgore Trout important?

13. How does Vonnegut portray the "military manner" of thinking?

14. Is Billy Pilgrim a Christ figure? Explain.

Test 2

1. Bernard V. O'Hare is embarrassed when _____ Vonnegut tries to talk to him about the war because
   I. he wants to forget about the war
   II. his wife will be mad if he talks to Vonnegut
   III. he doesn't think the war should be exploited for money
   A. I and II only   B. I and III only
   C. I, II, and III

2. Roland Weary keeps Billy with him because _____ he
   A. likes tormenting Billy
   B. will look like a hero for saving Billy's life
   C. likes Billy

3. When Billy sees the crippled men selling _____ phony magazine subscriptions, he
   A. calls the Better Business Bureau
   B. buys a subscription out of pity
   C. weeps for them and their boss

4. The Tralfamadorians take no notice of free _____ will because they
   A. see all time all at once
   B. are determinists
   C. think Earthlings are stupid

5. The English POWs have an easy time of it _____
   because
   I. the Germans adore them
   II. they are all officers
   III. there has been a clerical error
   A. I, II, and III   B. II and III only
   C. I and III only

6. Billy's "vision of hell" refers to _____
   A. Dresden after the bombing
   B. the latrine at the prison camp
   C. the zoo on Tralfamadore

7. Howard W. Campbell, Jr., describes _____
   American POWs as being
   A. "clever, graceful, quiet"
   B. "the most self-pitying, least fraternal,
      and dirtiest of all"
   C. "the great explainers"

8. Dresden was an "open city" because _____
   A. it was so beautiful
   B. there were hospitals there
   C. it had no military value

9. The barbershop quartet upsets Billy because _____
   A. they remind him of the guards in
      Dresden
   B. their songs are tasteless
   C. they are terrible singers

10. Billy goes to New York to: _____
    A. visit an old war buddy
    B. go to a pornography store
    C. get on a TV or radio show

11. What are the problems Vonnegut had in writing his
    book about Dresden?

12. What effect does the war have on Billy Pilgrim?

13. How is time presented in *Slaughterhouse-Five*?

14. Discuss Vonnegut's attitude towards machines, giving examples.

ANSWERS

Test 1

1. C   **2.** C   **3.** B   **4.** A   **5.** C   **6.** B
7. B   **8.** C   **9.** B   **10.** A

11. For Billy the Tralfamadorians function as superior beings whose philosophy enables him to come to terms with his life. They give him Montana to enable him to "start the world over again" as a new Adam with his Eve. For Vonnegut the Tralfamadorians provide an opportunity to comment, from an "alien" perspective, on the absurdity of modern life and the illusions that human beings hold dear. The Tralfamadorians see all time all at once, and so to them free will—the idea that we make our own choices in life—does not exist. To them we are like bugs trapped in amber because past, present, and future are all fixed.

12. Vonnegut himself wrote science fiction stories for magazines, and for many years he failed to win much of an audience for his writings. Perhaps Kilgore Trout is Vonnegut's caricature of himself. Or perhaps Vonnegut feared that he would turn into a bitter and crazed man like Kilgore Trout if he didn't get some recognition as a writer.

Vonnegut uses paraphrases of Trout's novels to satirize American values. *The Gutless Wonder,* which is about a robot who becomes popular when his bad breath is cleared up, parodies the inane mentality of advertising. In *The Big Board* an Earthling couple's greed provides entertainment in an alien zoo.

Finally, Trout's novels furnish Billy Pilgrim with the material and the inspiration for his therapeutic fantasies, and they help him to remember consciously his Dresden experience.

13. The most primitive example of this is Roland Weary with his pathetic fantasies of heroism and deep friendships forged in battle. More sophisticated are the English officers in the German prison camp, who make war look "stylish and fun." But Vonnegut's exemplar of the "military manner" of thinking is Professor Rumfoord. Rumfoord's wives are mere trophies of his virility, he is a staunch social Darwinist who believes that only the strong should survive, and he thinks that the men who bombed Dresden, not the victims, are the ones who should be pitied.

Vonnegut also quotes extensively from military writings and speeches, usually selecting passages that seem to him to be the most absurd.

14. There are numerous references to Jesus in *Slaughterhouse-Five*. Two novels by Kilgore Trout reexamine the New Testament story, and the horse pitiers croon like Jesus's friends taking his body down from the cross. Billy is twice directly associated with Jesus: he is "crucified" on a cross-brace in the boxcar, and the Christmas carol "Away in the Manger" is said to describe Billy's inability to weep.

In some ways Billy's story parallels the life of Jesus. He tries to preach a message of hope and peace, but few people are ready for it. And in a vision he sees himself being assassinated for trying to change the world.

Test 2
1. C   2. B   3. C   4. A   5. A   6. B
7. B   8. C   9. A   10. C

11. Some of Vonnegut's problems had to do with the

nature of writing itself. Writing distorts events by making them plot elements in a story, and it turns actual people into characters. This process in turn dehumanizes the writer himself. Beyond this, writing cannot make sense of an atrocity.

Vonnegut saw ethical problems too. Another antiwar book would be worse than pointless because all war stories encourage war. Vonnegut's Dresden experience was absurd, so to make sense of it by writing a "good story" would be a lie.

Vonnegut found that he could most truthfully present his story if he adopted a point of view that combined the innocent perspective of the "baby" he was during the war with the embarrassed hindsight of the adult writing the story years later.

12. All of Billy Pilgrim's problems with life stem from his experiences in World War II. Exhaustion, exposure and hunger take their toll on his body, but far worse is the psychological damage he suffers as a result of witnessing the destruction of Dresden. Three years after coming home from the war he has a nervous breakdown, and commits himself to a mental hospital, where he meets others like himself who have "found life meaningless, partly because of what they had seen in the war," and who are "alarmed by the outside world."

He seems to recover, and goes on to marry and raise a family, as well as becoming a prosperous optometrist and prominent citizen in his hometown of Ilium, New York. But every once in a while he falls asleep on the job, and has fits of weeping that he cannot explain. These symptoms indicate that something is still bothering him, no matter how normal he appears to everyone else.

Finally, while in the hospital recuperating from a near-fatal plane crash, Billy starts putting together a complicated fantasy to help him cope with the horror of his war experience. This fantasy—which involves reorganizing his life through time-travel and imagining wise and kindly aliens who set him up in a new Garden of Eden with his dream-lover Montana Wildhack—lets Billy escape the meaninglessness of modern existence into a re-invented life that makes sense.

13. Billy Pilgrim believes that he is "unstuck in time," living his life out of sequence, jumping around from one period of his life to another in no apparent order. Actually there is one period—the six months from December 1944 to May 1945, when he was a soldier and then a POW in Europe during World War II—which he does experience more or less from beginning to end. Although there are frequent interruptions for visits to the past, the future, and his fantasy about the Tralfamadorians and Montana Wildhack, Billy always returns to the war pretty much where he left off.

Billy is trying to reinvent his life by reorganizing his memories and adding fantasy. He does this by fitting all the other events in his life into the sequence of his war experiences, and thus is finally able to come to terms with what he saw and heard and did in those six months.

Vonnegut suggests that Billy's time-travel is analogous to the way memory and fantasy work in our lives. Memory is a kind of time-travel into the past; fantasy takes us into the future. By structuring the novel the way he does, he is thus able to describe directly our subjective (internal) experience of the passage of time, which is so different from the objective (external) time of clocks and calendars.

14. There are few machines in *Slaughterhouse-Five* that aren't harmful to people. The most obvious examples are weapons: the bombers that devastate Dresden and

Roland Weary's antitank gun, which ironically murders its operators by drawing enemy fire. Other machines destroy people accidentally. An elevator squashes a man who gets his ring caught in the door, and Valencia dies when her Cadillac poisons her with carbon monoxide fumes.

To make a point Vonnegut often describes living things mechanistically, as when the group of POWs is said to be "essentially a liquid which could be induced to flow slowly toward cooing and light," or when Billy's spine is called a "tube" with all of his important "wires" in it. In reverse, machines are often given human attributes: trains full of POWs say hello to each other across the rail yard, and the boxcar becomes "a single organism which ate and drank and excreted through its ventilators."

Term Paper Ideas and other Topics for Writing

Themes

1. Show how *Slaughterhouse-Five* functions as an anti-war book. Is the argument effective?

2. Compare *Slaughterhouse-Five* with Stephen Crane's *The Red Badge of Courage* and/or Ernest Hemingway's *A Farewell to Arms*. How is Vonnegut's message different from or similar to these works?

3. Most people agree that Nazism was truly evil. Was the bombing of Dresden therefore justified?

4. How is authority presented in *Slaughterhouse-Five*?

5. As expressed in *Slaughterhouse-Five*, what does Vonnegut see as the possibility for a meaningful life in the modern world?

6. Does *Slaughterhouse-Five* state that art is necessary to make sense of life? How?

7. In *Slaughterhouse-Five*, how and why do the demands of storytelling distort real events?

8. From *Slaughterhouse-Five* would you conclude that Vonnegut is a feminist, or is his admiration for women a form of "male chauvinism"?

9. It has been said that machines make great servants but terrible masters. How is this idea expressed in *Slaughterhouse-Five*?

10. How does Vonnegut present the contrast between the "realism" of social Darwinism and the "idealism" of Jesus's Sermon on the Mount in *Slaughterhouse-Five*?

Characters
1. Compare Billy's wife Valencia, Montana Wildhack, and Mary O'Hare as representative females.

2. In what sense is *Slaughterhouse-Five* an autobiographical novel?

Style
1. Discuss Vonnegut's use of imagery in *Slaughterhouse-Five*.

2. Does Vonnegut's slangy, conversational tone trivialize or strengthen the book's serious points?

3. Is the "telegraphic schizophrenic" style of *Slaughterhouse-Five* essential to the book's message, or is it merely a clever device?

Vonnegut's Other Writings

1. Vonnegut says that *Slaughterhouse-Five* and *Breakfast of Champions* were originally one book. Why might he have separated them?

2. Discuss Vonnegut's treatment of the free will vs. determinism theme in *Slaughterhouse-Five* and at least two of his other novels. Is he consistent in his view or does he change his mind on the subject?

Further Reading
CRITICAL WORKS

Aldridge, John W. *The American Novel and the Way We Live Now*. New York: Oxford University Press, 1983. Lumps Vonnegut with Thomas Pynchon and John Barth and finds fault with all of them.

Goldsmith, David H. *Kurt Vonnegut: Fantasist of Fire and Ice*. Bowling Green, Ohio: Bowling Green University Popular Press, 1972. A good overview of Vonnegut's vision and technique.

Hipkiss, Robert A. *The American Absurd: Pynchon, Vonnegut and Barth*. Port Washington, N.Y.: National University Publications Associated Faculty Press, 1984. Places Vonnegut in the larger literary tradition of the absurd, exemplified by such earlier European writers as Albert Camus and Samuel Beckett.

Karl, Frederick. *American Fictions: 1940–1980*. New York: Harper & Row, 1983. A distillation of the negative criticism leveled against Vonnegut over the years (pp. 344–347).

Klinkowitz, Jerome. *Kurt Vonnegut*. New York: Methuen, 1982. Good details on Vonnegut's life and some lively analysis of the novels.

Klinkowitz, Jerome, and John Somer, editors. *The Von-negut Statement*. New York: Delacorte, 1973. A collec-tion of essays on Vonnegut the public figure, the lit-erary figure, and the artist.

Lundquist, James. *Kurt Vonnegut*. New York: Ungar, 1977. Concentrates brilliantly on *Slaughterhouse-Five*.

Mayo, Clark. *Kurt Vonnegut: The Gospel from Outer Space*. San Bernardino, Cal.: R. Reginald/The Borgo Press, 1977. Good general commentary on all the novels.

Scholes, Robert. *The Fabulators*. New York: Oxford Uni-versity Press, 1967. A good description of black hu-mor and Vonnegut's place among his contemporaries.

Tanner, Tony. *City of Words: American Fiction, 1950–1970*. New York: Harper & Row, 1971. Clear and complete commentary on the novels, up to and including *Slaughterhouse-Five*.

AUTHOR'S OTHER WORKS

Player Piano. (Novel) 1952.

The Sirens of Titan. (Novel) 1959.

Mother Night. (Novel) 1961.

Canary in a Cathouse. (Stories) 1961.

Cat's Cradle. (Novel) 1963.

God Bless You, Mr. Rosewater. (Novel) 1965.

Welcome to the Monkey House. (Stories. All but one of the stories in *Canary in a Cathouse*, plus fourteen others) 1968.

Happy Birthday, Wanda June. (Play) 1971.

Between Time and Timbuktu. (Teleplay) 1972.

Breakfast of Champions. (Novel) 1973.

Wampeters, Foma and Granfalloons. (Essays) 1974.

Slapstick (Novel) 1976.

Jailbird. (Novel) 1979.

Sun Moon Star. (Children's book) 1980.

Palm Sunday. (Essays) 1981.
Deadeye Dick. (Novel) 1982.

Glossary

The number in parentheses that follows each entry is the number of the chapter in which the term first occurs in the novel.

Amber A clear resin, yellowish brown in color, in which accidentally trapped insects are sometimes found. (4)

Amoretti Cherubs or cupids; symbols of love. (6)

Barbershop quartet An ensemble of four male voices, singing popular songs in close harmony. Apparently an American invention of the 1890s. (7)

Battle of the Bulge Following the Allied invasion of Europe in June of 1944, the Germans launched a huge counteroffensive in December, inflicting many casualties. (2)

Céline Pen name of Louis-Ferdinand Auguste Destouches (1894–1961), a French novelist who became a Nazi sympathizer and was later tried as a war criminal. (1)

Delousing station Where parasites such as fleas, lice, and ticks were removed from POWs and their clothing. (4)

Dogtag A metal chip imprinted with a soldier's name, rank, and serial number and worn around his neck for identification. (5)

Dum-dums Bullets that explode on impact, causing much greater damage than ordinary bullets (2)

"Eheu, fugaces labuntur anni" Latin for "Alas, the fleeing years slip away," from an ode by the Roman poet Ovid. (1)

Fire-storm In Dresden, when the fires started by incendiary bombs joined together, they created "one big flame" that quickly exhausted the air immediately surrounding the city, creating a huge vacuum. Air from outside the bombing area was then sucked into the vacuum, causing gale-force winds and fanning the flames still further. (1)

Fourragère of snot and blutwurst and tobacco juice and Schnapps A fourragère is a French military decoration, a braid worn at the left shoulder. Blutwurst is the German word for blood sausage. Schnapps is strong liquor. (3)

Gideon Bible An American "missionary" group called the Gideons place Bibles in hotel and motel rooms throughout the United States. (1)

Goethe, Johann Wolfgang von German poet and dramatist (1749–1832). He is to the Germans what Shakespeare is to the English. (1)

Green Berets The special forces division of the American army during the war in Vietnam. The Green Berets took on the most difficult and dangerous assignments. John Wayne produced and starred in a movie glorifying their exploits. (2)

Hiroshima The Japanese city on which the first atomic bomb was dropped on August 6, 1945. (1)

Hitler, Adolf Born Adolf Schicklgruber (1889–1945), he helped form the National Socialist (Nazi) party in Germany and became head of government in 1933. Started World War II by invading Poland in September 1939. (4)

Hors de combat In French, out of the combat or disabled. (title page)

Howitzer A short, light cannon. (2)

Ilium, New York An imaginary city in upstate New York, also the setting of Vonnegut's novel *Player Piano*. Also, the Greek name for the ancient city of Troy, site of the Trojan War. (There is a city named Troy in upstate New York, but most readers think Ilium is more like the city of Schenectady (near Troy), where Vonnegut once worked.) (2)

Jerry The English nickname for German soldiers. Americans tended to call Germans "krauts." (5)

John Birch Society An extreme right-wing (conservative) political group, strongly anti-Communist and racist in its ideology. (3)

Lions Club A men's civic organization, similar to the Jaycees, Kiwanis, and Rotary. (3)

Luftwaffe The German air force in World War II. (1)

Maori Polynesian people who inhabited New Zealand when Europeans arrived; New Zealand had close ties to Great Britain at the time of World War II. (10)

Menjou, Adolphe A suave character actor in American movies during the thirties and forties, who always sported a well-groomed moustache. (10)

Mongolian idiot A person with Downs' syndrome, a congenital defect characterized by mental retardation. The name "Mongoloid" comes from the almond-shaped eyes characteristic of the syndrome. (9)

Mustard gas A poison gas ($(ClCH_2CH_2)_2S$), used in World War I. (1)

Mutt and Jeff Popular comic strip characters; Jeff is tall and skinny, Mutt is short and squat. (1)

Nazi A member of Hitler's political party, the National Socialists. The name comes from the German sound of the first two syllables of the party's German name, *Nati*onalsocialistische Partei. (1)

"The Pirates of Penzance" A comic opera by the famous English team of lyricist W. S. Gilbert and composer Arthur Sullivan. (5)

Roethke, Theodore An American poet (1908–1963). (1)

Saint Elmo's fire The flamelike radiance that sometimes can be seen surrounding the prominent parts of a ship in stormy weather. (3)

Salmon roe Salmon eggs, better known as red caviar. (8)

Spastic The appearance of prolonged and uncontrollable muscle spasms, usually the result of brain damage. (2)

"The Spirit of '76" A famous patriotic painting of the American Revolutionary War, depicting two grown men and a boy, wounded and ragged, marching heroically. (2)

Three Musketeers Principal characters in the novel *The Three Musketeers* by Alexandre Dumas père; their motto was "All for one, and one for all." (2)

Thumbscrew An instrument of torture consisting of a ring into which the thumb is inserted and a screw that is then tightened gradually, until the bones are shattered. (2)

Trifocals Eyeglasses containing three separate lenses for each eye, one for far distance, one for middle distance, and one for close work. (3)

V-1's and V-2's Rockets designed by German scientists for bombing Britain without risking airplanes. (9)

Vietnam Southeast Asian country where America fought an undeclared war for some ten years in the 1960s and 1970s. (3)

WACS, WAVES, SPARS, and WAFS Women's divisions of the armed services during World War II. (5)

The Critics

On Vonnegut

One thing is apparent from the start in reading Vonnegut: he is an enthusiast of sentimental detachment, a Pinball Wizard of cosmic cool who, through the charm of his style and the subtle challenge of his ideas, encourages us to adopt his interplanetary midwestern viewpoint and to believe once again in such radically updated values as love, compassion, humility, and conscience. He is a dervish of paradox as he suggests in his extended fables that we must learn to maintain happy illusions over villainous ones, that the best truth is a comforting lie, and that if there is any purpose to human history, it is best understood as a joke—at our expense.

—James Lundquist, *Kurt Vonnegut,* 1977

Billy Pilgrim . . . is the product of Vonnegut's unquestioning attitude toward extremely complicated historical elements, which, for the sake of a "morality play," he simplifies. . . . Its intentions pure, its morality innocent, its attitudes beyond ethical reproach, *Slaughterhouse-Five* nevertheless turns human behavior and history into molasses.

—Frederick Karl, *American Fictions: 1940–1980,* 1983

Vonnegut consciously chooses a stance of naivete and wonder—the "child-like"—as well as sentiment and self-pity—the "childish." In many ways, he is sensitive and profound; in others, he remains a blurb-writer, still doing public relations work, but now for himself.

—Clark Mayo, *Kurt Vonnegut: The Gospel from Outer Space,* 1977

On *Slaughterhouse-Five*

It is the tone of the novel rather than the overt statements of the author which leads one to believe that Vonnegut has finally washed the horror and guilt of Dresden from his mind and has come to accept the previously unacceptable—man's capacity for evil, the tongue-in-cheek way this evil seems to be directed, or abetted, by some exterior force, and the helplessness of the individual to do much about either. Billy is battered but alive, and will continue to live. These facts, and the comfort they evidently give Billy's creator (his literary creator) produce the exact opposite of a fatalistic mood in the novel; if anything the book is sentimental.

—David H. Goldsmith, *Kurt Vonnegut: Fantasist of Fire and Ice,* 1972

Can one afford to ignore the ugly moments in life

by concentrating on the happy ones? On the other hand, can one afford *not* to? Perhaps the fact of the matter is that conscience simply cannot cope with events like the concentration camps and the Dresden air-raid, and the more general demonstration by the war of the utter valuelessness of human life. Even to try to begin to care adequately would lead to an instant and irrevocable collapse of consciousness. Billy Pilgrim, Everyman, needs his fantasies to offset such facts.

—Tony Tanner, *City of Words*, 1971

Fantasy, Science Fiction, and Time

Vonnegut uses science fiction in *The Sirens of Titan* and *Slaughterhouse-Five* to open up the question of a purpose in the universe, the problem of man's morality in an amoral universe, and the adjunctive question of free will. The extraterrestrial domain in his novels shows what present scientific and social Earth trends may become, offers a detached perspective on Earth's condition as we look at it from the viewpoint of extraterrestrial beings, and suggests alternate modes of perception that might be opposed to our normal human view of ourselves. Vonnegut makes it very clear that space and technological invention are not escapes from Earth's problems. They magnify those problems rather than reducing them.

—Robert A. Hipkiss, *The American Absurd*, 1984

Through the constant movement back and forth in time that constitutes Vonnegut's narrative, we see Billy becoming his history, existing all at once, as if he is an electron. And this gives the novel a structure that is, to directly state the analogy, atomic. Billy whirls around the central fact of Dresden, the planes of his orbits constantly intersecting, and where he has been, he will be.

—James Lundquist, *Kurt Vonnegut*, 1977

NOTES

NOTES

NOTES

NOTES

NOTES

NOTES

NOTES

NOTES

9 780764 191237